Vocabulary skill	Grammar	Writing skill	Writing task	video	Study skills
Reporting verbs	Modals	Using compound sentences	Describing a special dish in your country	Living with supermarkets	Reflective learning journals
Suffixes that change verbs into nouns	Verbs of compulsion and prohibition	Brainstorming: Organizing your ideas in a chart	Describing your community's rules	Safety and freedom	Brainstorming and essay planning
Scientific terms with Latin and Greek roots	Passive voice	Using a variety of sentence types	Describing an amateur discovery	Crowding out our brains	Improving reading comprehension
Comparing and contrasting	Comparatives and superlatives	Complex sentences	Comparing consumer behavior	Living larger, living longer	Common features of all academic writing
Finding synonyms	The past progressive	Combining facts and dates	Writing a personal statement	Winning	Editing your own work
Opinion adverbs	Present conditionals	Expanding notes into summaries	Writing a summary	Life under pressure	Referencing and plagiarism
Verb and preposition collocations	The present perfect simple	Developing paragraphs	Describing a common fear	Fear of animals	Ways of working with others
Dictionary skills	Defining relative clauses	Definition paragraphs	Describing a study subject	Bad news	Reviewing material
Cause and effect	The passive: present and past perfect	Using statistics	Writing about a water issue	Water politics	Forming a study group
Finding meaning from synonyms or antonyms	Indirect quotation	Presenting a claim	Writing a persuasive essay	Just say yes	Critical thinking when writing

To the Student

Academic success requires so much more than memorizing facts. It takes skills. This means that a successful student can both learn and think critically.

Skillful gives you:

- Skills for learning about a wide variety of topics from different angles and from different academic areas
- Skills you need to succeed when reading and listening to these texts
- Skills you need to succeed when writing for and speaking to different audiences
- Skills for critically examining the issues presented by a speaker or a writer
- Study skills for learning and remembering the English language and important information.

To successfully use this book, use these strategies:

- **Come to class prepared to learn** This means that you should show up well fed, well rested, and prepared with the proper materials (paper, pen, textbook, completed homework, and so on).
- **Ask questions and interact** Learning a language is not passive. You need to actively participate. Help your classmates, and let them help you. It is easier to learn a language with other people.
- **Practice!** Do each exercise a few times, with different partners. Memorize and use new language. Use the *Skillful* digital component to develop the skills presented in the Student's Book. Complete the additional activities on your computer outside of class to make even more progress.
- **Review your work** Look over the the skills, grammar, and vocabulary from previous units. Study a little bit each day, not just before tests.
- **Be an independent learner, too** Look for opportunities to study and practice English outside of class, such as reading for pleasure and using the Internet in English. Find and then share information about the different unit topics with your classmates.

Remember that learning skills, like learning a language, takes time and practice. Be patient with yourself, but do not forget to set goals. Check your progress and be proud of your success!

I hope you enjoy using *Skillful*!

Dorothy E. Zemach
Series Consultant

Skillful

Reading&Writing

Student's Book

2

Authors: Louis Rogers & Jennifer Wilkin
Series Consultant: Dorothy E. Zemach

Contents

	Reading texts	Reading skills		
UNIT 1 **Nourishment** Page 7	1 Food as communication **Cultural studies** 2 Farms of the future **Technology**	**Before you read** Previewing **Close reading** Scanning	**Global** Identifying the purpose of parts of a text	
UNIT 2 **Community** Page 17	1 Living by the rules **Sociology** 2 Ants: master collaborators **Sociobiology**	**Global** Skimming	**Close** Note taking: Mapping	
UNIT 3 **Space** Page 27	1 Discovered by amateurs **Astronomy** 2 Close encounters **Astronomy**	**Close** Identifying definitions	**Global** Creating a text plan	
UNIT 4 **Scale** Page 37	1 The superconsumer generation **Sociology** 2 The sky's the limit **Current affairs**	**Global** Summarizing	**Close** Pronoun referents	
UNIT 5 **Success** Page 47	1 What does it take to be successful? **Business studies** 2 Did they just get lucky? **Popular science**	**Global** Identifying main ideas	**Close** Identifying cause and effect	
UNIT 6 **Pressure** Page 57	1 The stresses and strains of work **Business studies** 2 Rich and famous **Sociology**	**Close** Taking notes: Using your own words	**Global** Identifying tone **Close** Researching an essay	
UNIT 7 **Fear** Page 67	1 Fears, reactions, coping **Psychology** 2 Superhuman powers **Physiology**	**Global** Using topic sentences	**Close** Identifying supporting details	
UNIT 8 **Stories** Page 77	1 National hero **History** 2 Mixed memories **Psychology**	**Global** Fact and opinion	**Close** Identifying reasons	
UNIT 9 **Water** Page 87	1 Fresh water delivery **Technology** 2 The world's largest garbage dump **Ecology**	**Close** Reading charts and graphs	**Close** Finding supporting evidence for main ideas	
UNIT 10 **Persuasion** Page 97	1 Charisma **Psychology** 2 The healing power of persuasion **Medicine**	**Close** Identifying types of supporting details	**Global** Bridge sentences	

Welcome to *Skillful*!

Each *Skillful* unit has ten pages and is divided into two main sections: reading skills and writing skills.

Reading

The reading skills section always comes first and starts with a *Discussion point* to lead you in to the unit topic.

There are then two reading texts for you to practice your reading skills on. There are activities to practice your global reading skills and your close reading skills, as well as opportunities to critically examine the ideas in the texts. Key academic vocabulary from the text is presented on the page so you can see essential terms to learn.

Vocabulary skills also give you the chance to develop the ways in which you learn and remember vocabulary from the reading texts.

FEARS, REACTIONS, COPING

1 Many people have a fear of things like snakes, spiders, heights, water, and small enclosed spaces. If many people have the same fears, how do we all develop them?

2 If you think about the time when we did not live in houses, but alongside nature, we faced many more dangers from animals. We have developed a response to situations that might cause us harm, such as a bite from a poisonous snake or a bite from a dog. Of course, not all fears are innate.

3 For example, if you see someone almost drown, you may react by developing a fear of water. Or, if a parent has a fear of heights, it is quite common for their children to also develop a fear of heights. The reason for this is not genetic; it is simply because children learn behavior and attitudes from their parents.

4 To answer this question, we have to define what is meant by phobia. While almost everyone has a fear of something, whether it is spiders or flying, a fear is only classified as a phobia by psychologists if it is so serious it affects your daily life. According to the Anxiety Disorders Association of America, 19 million Americans (around 6 percent of the population) have specific phobias, such as crossing bridges or going through tunnels. Another 15 million (around 5 percent) have a social phobia such as public speaking. Unfortunately, those who have one phobia are likely to have others too.

5 Because many fears are learned during our lives, we simply have to unlearn these feelings. If people confront their fear in a gradual way, they can learn to control how they react to the situation and not panic. It might not cure the fear completely, but it will probably help people to cope better.

Writing

The writing section has two main parts: grammar and writing skills. You can find information on each of these in boxes on the page and these give essential information on these skills. At the end of this section is a writing task for you to put the ideas from the texts and the skills from the writing section into practice. Use the checklist on page 109 to see how well your partner has completed the task.

The final page in the unit focuses on study skills which will help you to achieve academic success. Some of these pages come from *The Study Skills Handbook* by Stella Cottrell, while others are engaging scenarios for you to read and reflect on.

Using *Skillful* gives you everything you need for academic success.

Good luck!

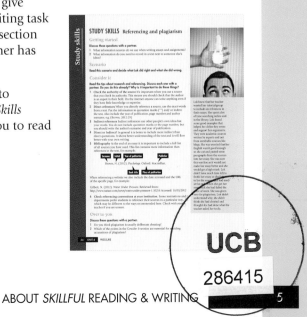

Introduction

Each *Skillful* Student's Book comes with a code in the back of the book that gives you free access to the accompanying digital component. The digital component encourages a more interactive and engaging learning environment and is very simple to access. Just go to www.skillfuldigibooks.com, and follow the step-by-step instructions to get started!

The first time you access the digital component you will need an Internet connection, but after this it is possible to work offline if you wish.

Digibook

This contains all the same content as your printed Student's Book, but you can use it on your computer, enabling easier navigation through the pages, a zoom function to create better student focus, and a personal annotation resource for helpful classroom notes.

Skillful Practice

You can either complete the extra activities as you go through the Digibook via the interactive icons, or you can find them all in one place in the *Skillful* Practice area. Here you will find a variety of activities to practice all the new skills and language you have learned in the Student's Book, including vocabulary, grammar, and skills-based activities.

There are also additional productive tasks and video activities linked to the unit topics.

If you complete any of the extra activities while you are online, your score will be recorded in your markbook so that your teacher can track your progress. If you work offline, your scores will be stored and transferred to your markbook the next time you connect.

Whether online or offline, in the classroom or on the move, the *Skillful* digital component allows you to access and use its content while encouraging interactive learning and effortless self-study.

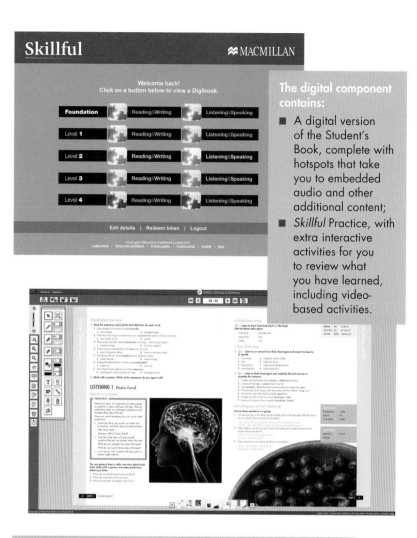

The digital component contains:

- A digital version of the Student's Book, complete with hotspots that take you to embedded audio and other additional content;
- *Skillful* Practice, with extra interactive activities for you to review what you have learned, including video-based activities.

The Digibook also contains lots of hotspots that link to additional content not in your printed Student's Book:

- Audio files for all of the reading texts
- Useful language to support discussion activities
- Dictionary definitions for the *Academic Keywords*
- Unit checklists so you can monitor how well you are progressing through the course.

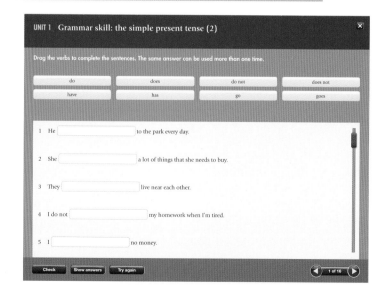

Nourishment

READING	Previewing
	Scanning
	Identifying the purpose of parts of a text
VOCABULARY	Reporting verbs
WRITING	Using compound sentences
GRAMMAR	Modals

Discussion point

Discuss these questions with a partner.

1   Look at the picture. Describe what you can see.

2   What kind of foods do you enjoy eating? Are they local products, or from other countries?

   I enjoy eating ...
   It comes from ...

3   What foods have special meaning in your culture? When do you eat them?

   Some of the foods that have a special meaning in my culture are ...
   We eat ... to celebrate ...

Vocabulary preview

Match the words in bold with a word or phrase with a similar meaning.

1   Giving money is a popular Chinese New Year **tradition**.
2   Every piece of jewelery she makes is **unique**; you'll never see two that are the same.
3   The new businesses brought **prosperity** to the town.
4   On our country's flag, white **symbolizes** peace.
5   The group was not successful because there was no **unity** amongst its members—they were always disagreeing.
6   Rice is one of the world's most important sources of **nutrition**.
7   People living in large **urban** areas often experience problems with traffic and air pollution.
8   He was a very **prominent** and well-respected member of the community.

a   unlike anything or anyone else
b   relating to towns and cities
c   custom
d   represents
e   wealth
f   important and well-known
g   food that is necessary for life and health
h   state of cooperation, agreement, or friendship between people or countries

READING 1   Food as communication

Before you read

> **PREVIEWING**
>
> Previewing key parts of a text before you read makes it easier for you to understand its main ideas. Look at the pictures, read the title, introduction, and any headings in the text, and skim over the passage. Then think about the topic and what you already know about it. When you have a sense of what the text is about *before* you read, you should be able to understand and remember it better.

Preview *Food as communication* and answer the questions.

1   Where do you think this text comes from?
   a   a daily newspaper
   b   a magazine called *World Culture*
   c   a magazine called *World of Nature*

2   What is the main idea?
   a   the importance of food in culture
   b   the high cost of eating well
   c   the importance of healthy eating

3   What do you already know about the topic?

4   What do you hope to learn from the text?

Global reading

Read *Food as communication*. Match the sentences with the paragraph they best summarize.

a   Food is important in many New Year celebrations around the world.
b   Around the world, food is important in welcoming ceremonies for young children.
c   Food can bring people together.
d   Food is a way of communicating.

Close reading

> **SCANNING**
>
> Scanning is a technique used when you are looking for specific information. It is important for you to practice this skill as academic reading is usually for a specific purpose such as answering an essay question. This skill will help you find information more quickly.

Complete the chart with information from the text.

Food	Culture or country	Significance or meaning
1 bread	*worldwide*	
2	*southern U.S.*	*prosperity or wealth*
3 vasilopita		*success in the new year*
4	*China*	*to welcome a new baby*
5 butter and sugar		
6 various foods / grain of rice		*to protect the baby from hunger*
7 round foods	*worldwide*	

Food as communication

ACADEMIC KEYWORDS

communication	(n)	/kəˌmjunɪˈkeɪʃ(ə)n/
significance	(n)	/sɪgˈnɪfɪkəns/
symbolic	(adj)	/sɪmˈbɑlɪk/

1 We usually understand when someone speaks or writes to us, and many gestures and facial expressions have meaning, too. But have you ever considered what and how we eat as a form of communication? Food serves this purpose in two fundamental ways. In many cultures, people share food at mealtimes. Sharing bread or other foods is a common human tradition that can promote unity and trust. Food can also have a specific meaning, and play a prominent role in a family or culture's celebrations or traditions. The foods we eat—and when and how we eat them—are often unique to a particular culture, or may even differ between rural and urban areas within one country.

2 In most cultures, bread represents nourishment. It is also one of the most commonly shared foods in the world. Sharing bread, whether during a special occasion or at the family dinner table, is a common symbol of companionship and togetherness. In fact, the word *companion* comes from the Latin roots *com-* (together) and *panis* (bread). Many cultures also celebrate birthdays and marriages with elaborately decorated cakes that are cut and shared among the guests. Early forms of cake were simply a kind of bread, so this tradition has its roots in the custom of sharing bread.

3 Food also plays an important role in many New Year celebrations. In the southern United States, pieces of cornbread represent blocks of gold for prosperity in the new year. In Greece, people share a special cake called *vasilopita*. A coin is baked into the cake, which signifies success in the new year for the person who receives it. Most of the foods eaten during the Chinese New Year have symbolic significance. Sometimes this is based on their shape; for instance, long noodles symbolize long life. The symbolism can also be based on the sound of the word in Chinese; for example, people give out oranges because the word for "orange" sounds like the word for "wealth".

4 Food can also be part of a ceremony. For example, many cultures have ceremonies to celebrate the birth of a child, and food can play a significant role. In China, when a baby is one month old, families name and welcome their child in a celebration that includes giving red-colored eggs to guests. In Afghanistan, parents feed babies butter and sugar for the first six days of life to symbolize cleansing. In a ceremony around 100 days after a child's birth, Japanese families symbolically "feed" the baby by putting different kinds of food to its lips, and sometimes putting a single grain of rice in its mouth. This ritual expresses their hope that the baby will never be hungry. In many cultures, round foods such as grapes, pomegranates, bread, and moon cakes are eaten at welcome celebrations to symbolize family unity.

5 Nutrition is essential for life, so it is not surprising that food is such an important part of different cultures around the world. The food people eat during celebrations and ceremonies can symbolize many things, but sharing food is one custom that almost all humans have in common.

Developing critical thinking

Discuss these questions in a group.

1 Which foods are shared in your culture? Why?

In our culture, we share ... because ...

2 Many of the food traditions mentioned in the text are very old. Why do you think they are still important today?

Food traditions are important because ...

READING 2 Farms of the future

Before you read

Discuss these questions with a partner.

1 What are some of the reasons that food is transported over long distances?

2 What are the advantages or disadvantages of doing this?

Global reading

IDENTIFYING THE PURPOSE OF PARTS OF A TEXT

Usually different parts of a text perform different functions. Identifying the purpose of different parts of a text can help you recognize the structure and understand its overall purpose. Some common functions are listed below.

- **Introduce the topic** This is the first paragraph in which a new idea is mentioned.
- **Report data** Authors often group the most important figures and statistics together in one paragraph.
- **Explain facts** These paragraphs give real, true information rather than opinion, argument, or speculation. Authors often establish the facts of a situation *before* presenting opinion, argument, or speculation.
- **Give supporting information** These paragraphs present examples and other information to support arguments or to give context to the topic.
- **Present an argument** These paragraphs group together all the arguments on one side of an issue.
- **Present another side of an issue** A well-balanced text presents more than one side of an issue. Even if the author is biased they will often present opposing arguments to make the text appear neutral.

Read *Farms of the future*. Circle the purpose of each section of the text.

Paragraph	Purpose
1	present another side / report data / introduce the topic
2	report data / introduce the topic / present an argument
3	explain facts / give supporting information / present another side
4–5	present an argument / report data / explain facts
6–7	give supporting information/ present the other side / report data
8	present an argument / report data / explain facts
9	(conclusion)

Close reading

Read *Farms of the future* again and write *T* (true) or *F* (false).

1 The world's population is 9.1 billion. _____
2 Environmental health experts support vertical farming. _____
3 Rooftop farming is cheap. _____
4 Vertical farming would improve food safety. _____
5 Natural sunlight is sufficient on a skyscraper farm. _____
6 Thanet Earth produces 20% of U.K. lettuces. _____

ACADEMIC KEYWORDS		
approach	(n)	/əˈprəʊtʃ/
minimal	(adj)	/ˈmɪnɪm(ə)l/
prominent	(adj)	/ˈprɒmɪnənt/

1 Skyscrapers are the ultimate symbol of urban life. City dwellers are used to seeing tall office buildings, multistory five star hotels, and apartment towers with thousands of residents. Farms, on the other hand, are associated with rural life. However, there are experts who think that some skyscrapers should become farms in order to meet the increasing food needs of our planet.

2 By 2050, some social scientists suggest, almost 80% of the Earth's population could live in cities. In addition, the human population could increase to 9.1 billion people during that time, yet the amount of land available for farming will be the same. If current farming practices don't change by the middle of this century, one prominent expert claims, we will need an area of new land larger than Brazil to produce enough food for the planet.

3 Vertical farms, where urban farmers could grow crops like wheat and rice in environmentally friendly skyscrapers, could be the solution. In spite of concerns over high costs, environmental health experts want to make these urban farms a reality and use these skyscrapers to grow crops. They believe that we can increase food production by changing our thinking from *out* to *up*.

4 Vertical farms would have many advantages, supporters say. Vertically grown food would be cultivated with minimal effects on the environment.

Unlike traditional farming, vertical farming would not force animals out of their habitats by taking over large areas of land, nor would it pollute the air with the use of heavy farming equipment. Finally, in addition to creating more farmable land, vertical farms would reduce the cost and negative effects of transporting food over long distances.

5 Growing prosperity around the world has led to many people demanding and expecting that all foods are available all year round. Indoor farming could produce crops constantly, and crops would not suffer from weather-related problems like drought or flooding. In addition, the use of chemical pesticides for controlling insects would be minimal.

6 Critics of vertical farming point out that although crops growing in a tall glass building would get natural sunlight during the day, it wouldn't be enough. The plants closest to the windows would grow much more quickly than the plants further inside. The plants growing away from the windows may not produce as many or as high quality vegetables. For these reasons, vertical farms would need additional light sources.

7 Researchers have found that even in single-story greenhouses, artificial light is often needed for year-round crops. For example, Thanet Earth is a large indoor farming complex in the United Kingdom that produces 15% of the British lettuce crop. During the winter, the complex uses artificial light for 15 hours a day. Experts have concluded that generating enough solar energy to support growth requires an area about 20 times larger than the planting area. Therefore, natural light cannot be a workable solution for vertical farms.

8 Another way of growing fresh food year-round is to build urban farms on rooftops. This more practical approach may be more achievable than the idea of farms in glass skyscrapers, researchers suggest. However, rooftop farming is expensive, and unless people want to pay more for fresh, local food, the technique may not succeed in the marketplace.

9 Experts agree that innovative farming practices are needed to support the planet's need for more and more food at affordable costs, both to the farmer and to the consumer. Vertical and rooftop farms may be a small-scale answer, but the best ideas could be yet to come.

Farms *of the* future

Developing critical thinking

1 Discuss these questions in a group.

1 Do you think we need to produce more food or change our consumption habits? Why?

2 Are you willing to pay more for locally grown food? Why or why not? Think about the ideas in the box on the right.

I wouldn't pay more for local food because ...
I'd pay a little more for food grown near my home because ...

2 Think about the ideas from *Food as communication* and *Farms of the future* and discuss these questions in a group.

1 A traditional Sunday lunch in the West typically travels almost 13,000 miles to get to the dinner table. What traditional foods eaten in your country are now imported?

Nowadays we usually import most of our ... from ...

2 How can we share the world's food supply better? Think about the ideas in the box on the right.

We need to try new farming methods like ...

THINK ABOUT

air miles	quality
choice	transportation
distance	variety
freshness	

Vocabulary skill

REPORTING VERBS

Articles or scientific texts often cite research to support the writer's ideas. To introduce the results of the research, writers often use reporting verbs such as *claim*, *conclude*, *find*, *point out*, and *suggest* to present ideas. These can also indicate how certain the results of the research are.

The verbs *conclude*, *find*, and *point out* show that the writer has more confidence in the research:

Researchers have found that even in single-story greenhouses, artificial light is often needed for year-round crops.

The verbs *claim* and *suggest* show less certainty:

*By 2050, some social scientists **suggest**, almost 80% of the Earth's population could live in cities.*

THINK ABOUT

farming methods
international cooperation
trade

Read the sentences and decide whether they show more certainty or less certainty. Write *M* (more) or *L* (less).

1 Studies have suggested that rooftop gardens are a good solution for smaller urban areas. ____

2 Buying locally grown vegetables is better for the environment, experts point out. ____

3 One study concluded that vegetables that are transported far from where they are picked lose vital nutrients. ____

4 Some researchers claim that the benefits of using artificial light aren't enough to make it a good economical choice. ____

5 Researchers have found that even in single-story greenhouses, artificial light is often needed for year-round crops. ____

WRITING Describing a special dish in your country

You are going to learn about using compound sentences and modal verbs. You are then going to use these to write a paragraph describing special dishes eaten for celebrations or holidays in your country.

Writing skill

USING COMPOUND SENTENCES

Varying your sentence structure with compound sentences adds interest to your writing. A sentence with two or more independent clauses (clauses with a subject and a verb) is a compound sentence. The conjunctions most commonly used in compound sentences are *and*, *but*, and *so*.

| subject | verb | **conjunction** | subject | verb |

*Many cultures have ceremonies to celebrate the birth of a child, **and** food can play a prominent role.*

Nor and *yet* are also used to join independent clauses.

As a conjunction, *yet* has a similar function to *but*.

*Sharing food is a custom that almost all humans have in common, **yet** many countries don't have enough food while others have too much.*

Nor is used after a negative statement when adding another negative statement.

With *nor*, the first independent clause needs to have a verb in the negative. Invert the subject and verb after *nor*.

| subject | verb | **nor** | verb | subject |

*Indoor crops would not need a lot of chemical pesticides, **nor** would they suffer from weather-related problems.* (not *nor they would*)

1 **Look back at *Food as communication* and *Farms of the future*. Find an example of a compound sentence with each of the conjunctions listed below. Underline the subjects and highlight the verbs, then circle the conjunctions.**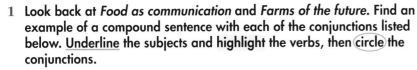

   1 and   (Text 2, paragraph 5)   **4** nor   (Text 2, paragraph 4)

   2 but   (Text 2, paragraph 9)   **5** yet   (Text 2, paragraph 2)

   3 so   (Text 1, paragraph 5)

2 **Circle the correct conjunction to complete these sentences.**

   1 It is more environmentally friendly to eat locally grown food, **nor / yet** many countries spend millions of dollars importing foods from thousands of miles away.

   2 Vertical farming would have many advantages, **but / and** one major drawback is that it would need to use artificial light.

   3 In many cultures, people eat symbolic foods to celebrate the new year, **and / so** food also plays an important role in welcoming ceremonies for babies in many countries.

   4 Rooftop farms do not require artificial light, **but / nor** do they pollute the air with the use of heavy farming equipment.

   5 The world's population is growing, **yet / so** we need more space to produce food.

3 **Write your own sentences about food. Use each conjunction from exercise 1 once.**

Grammar

MODALS

Modals have many uses. Three common uses are to talk about probability, make recommendations, and to show obligation. Study the forms:

Form	Example
Probability *Must* and *cannot* express strong certainty. subject + *must/cannot* + base form *May*, *might*, and *could* express an opinion that the writer thinks has a fair possibility of being true. subject + *might/could* + base form *Could* often expresses one possibility out of several.	Therefore, natural light **cannot** be a workable solution for vertical farms. The technique **might** not succeed in the marketplace. The human population **could** increase to 9.1 billion people by 2050.
Recommendation *Should* and *shouldn't* are used to make recommendations or suggestions. subject + *should* + base form	Urban populations **should** consider alternative sources of food.
Obligation *Need to* and *have to* are stronger and are used to show obligation. subject + *need to / have to* + base form *Cannot* shows negative obligation, but *don't have to* and *don't need to* shows no obligation.	The world **has to** find a viable solution to the potential food crisis. Food grown in vertical farms **doesn't have to** be transported very far.

1 **Look at these statements and decide if they express certainty (C), possibility (P), recommendation (R) or obligation (O).**

1 The consumption of food is dictated by rules in many cultures that visitors should be careful to observe. ____

2 In many countries, companies now have to follow rules regarding food advertising. ____

3 Reducing meat consumption could help lessen man's environmental impact. ____

4 Consumption patterns in developing countries cannot continue since they are not sustainable. ____

5 The world has to redress the balance of food distribution throughout the globe. ____

6 The world's population may start to fall again as families become smaller. ____

2 **Complete the sentences with the modals *need to, cannot, might, should*, and *have to* and the expressions in the box.**

> accept it   change   continue to feed   find a solution   grow a lot more food

1 If someone offers you food, you _____ because it symbolizes friendship.

2 If the world's population increases to 9.1 billion, we will _____ .

3 At the current rate of global population growth, we _____ the world's population with current farming methods.

4 Some cultural traditions _____ as the world becomes more globalized.

5 Supporters of vertical farming _____ to the light source problem if they want to make the idea a reality.

WRITING TASK

Write a short text describing a special dish, eaten in your culture on a special day.

BRAINSTORM

1   Read the paragraph and underline any compound sentences joined by *and*, *but*, or *so*. Highlight any modal verbs used. Are these used to express certainty, possibility, obligation, or recommendation?

Haggis

Haggis is a traditional Scottish dish eaten on Burn's night, an annual celebration to remember a famous Scottish poet. As with any dish, there are many different recipes; haggis for example, may be made with beef, but traditionally it is made with lamb. The customary ingredients include sheep's stomach, and the heart and lungs of a lamb. It is mixed with onions, oatmeal, and different herbs and spices. Apart from the spices, all these ingredients are found in Scotland, but nowadays many imported ingredients are used as well. Haggis is difficult to make, so it is usually prepared by a butcher or chef.

At a traditional Burns' night, a piper has to lead the haggis into the room, and the guests should then applaud the haggis. The host welcomes the guests, but a different person addresses the haggis. This person reads a Scottish poem before glasses are raised and everyone toasts the haggis. The dish is eaten with turnips and potatoes.

2   What special dishes does your family eat during holidays or special celebrations? Brainstorm a list and write your ideas in the chart.

Special dishes	Holiday or celebration

PLAN

Choose one special dish to write about. Answer the following questions as you plan your description.
1   What is the name of the dish?
2   What region of the country or world does the dish come from?
3   At what special celebration(s) or family event(s) is it eaten?
4   Who usually prepares the dish?
5   What are the key ingredients? Where are they grown or made?
6   How should you eat the dish?

WRITE

Using your answers to the questions above, write 2–3 paragraphs about a special dish in your family or culture. Use some compound sentences with *but, and, so, nor,* or *yet*. Pay attention to your use of modals. Your text should be 100 words long.

SHARE

Exchange paragraphs with a partner. Look at the checklist on page 109 and provide feedback to your partner.

REWRITE AND EDIT

Read your partner's comments. What could you change to make your writing better? Revise your text, then check it for errors. Write the final draft.

Reflective learning journals

by Stella Cottrell

In a strong notebook, or using your computer, start a reflective learning journal.

Why?

- Writing things down helps you to clarify your thoughts and emotions, to work out strategies, and to focus on your development and progress.
- A written record will help you see how you are progressing from week to week, and from semester to semester.

Who is it for?

For yourself—to help you focus on your own development.

What do you write?

Anything which helps you to reflect on:

- your feelings about the course, the lecturers, other students, your progress
- things you find difficult: challenges
- changes in your attitude or motivation
- how you tackle tasks—your strategies
- things you find out about yourself
- thoughts about how you learn best
- ideas that arise from your studies
- how different areas of study link up
- how your studies relate to real life.

> "… I can't believe the difference between my first essay (very bad!!!) and this one. Keeping an ideas book has helped."

> "I used to read the hardest books first— to be a 'real' student. Now I look for a simple overview first."

> "Why am I always late? I think it's because I always try to get somewhere on time, whereas I should think about getting there five minutes early—then I might be on time!"

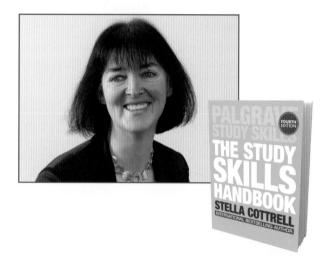

Other uses of reflective learning journals

As a basis for discussion

It can be helpful to discuss your journal or blog entries with other students on your course. How does their experience of the course compare with your own? Have they worked out strategies which might help you?

Preparing for tutorials

Go through the journal and make a list of issues that you want to discuss in your next tutorial. Put these in order of priority. If you have any problems, think through some possible options, so that the discussion with your tutor will be more focused.

Risky writing

Keeping a private journal helps to develop your writing. You can experiment with different styles if you want to. You can take risks. The journal is for your benefit—and for your eyes only. This may make a welcome change from writing to the demands of your course or tutors!

 Start now

How do you feel about starting your course? What challenges do you expect? How can you use your experiences to help you to meet these challenges?

READING	Skimming
	Note taking: Mapping
VOCABULARY	Word building:
	Suffixes that change
	verbs into nouns
WRITING	Brainstorming:
	Organizing your ideas
	in a chart
GRAMMAR	Verbs of compulsion
	and prohibition

Discussion point

Discuss these questions with a partner.

1 What different communities do you belong to? Think about your family, school, sports team, and neighborhood.

The communities I belong to are ...

2 What are some common rules for these communities? What are some rules specific to one community?

At my school, we have to ...
In my family, we are not allowed to ...

3 Why do we have rules? Why are they important?

We have rules because ...
I think rules are important in communities because ...

Vocabulary preview

For each word in bold, cross out the word that is *not* a synonym.

1	cheat	deceive	hurt	trick
2	compromise	give	negotiate	cooperate
3	conflicting	opposite	worthless	inconsistent
4	dictate	command	determine	announce
5	function	earn	work	operate
6	orderly	organized	disciplined	honest
7	punishment	discipline	rejection	penalty
8	reward	wealth	prize	award

READING 1   Living by the rules

Before you read

Work in groups. Do you agree with this quote? Why or why not? When is it acceptable for things to be unfair?

'Life is not fair. Get used to it.' (Bill Gates, founder of Microsoft®)

Global reading

SKIMMING

Skim reading is a useful skill to learn when you are preparing for academic study. You are likely to have a lot of texts to read, a lot of research to do, and not enough time to read everything on a topic. It is therefore often important to decide whether it is worth reading a text in greater detail. You can do this by skimming a text quickly to identify the main ideas using headings, sub-headings, and topic sentences to help give you a bigger picture.

1 Skim *Living by the rules* and check (✓) what it is about.

☐ how to make people's behavior fair

☐ why we have to compromise

☐ how to compromise in unfair situations

☐ why we have rules in our communities

2 Read *Living by the rules*. Highlight the main points as you read. Then compare with a partner. Did you highlight similar points? What are the differences?

Close reading

Scan back over *Living by the rules* and complete these sentences about the text.

1 A community is a group of people who are _____ by several factors.

2 When a situation is unfair, our brains respond with _____ feelings such as _____ and _____.

3 Social _____ are important in setting and following rules.

4 Internal controls are determined by our _____ and _____.

5 External controls include _____ and _____.

6 If we didn't have social controls, our communities would not _____ smoothly.

LIVING BY THE RULES ⊘ △ ⬡

What would life be like without rules? A recent study by Thurner, Szell, and Sinatra (2012) examined the behavior of avatars in an online world with no rules and found, perhaps surprisingly, that the lack of rules did not result in disorder. There was very little cheating or antisocial behavior. People organized themselves into groups and traded, communicated, and moved around much like people in the real world.

However, almost every community in the real world has some form of rules and some way of enforcing them. A community is a group of people who are united by a number of factors, including geography, language, and values that dictate acceptable behavior. So why do we have rules, and what makes people follow them?

Studies have suggested that the reason we don't like cheating and rule-breaking is because fairness is programmed into our brains. Tricomi et al (2010) have found that the brain reacts in a particular way when we feel we are being treated unfairly. The study identified a reaction in a specific part of the brain when test subjects were given less money than others. A fair situation makes our brains respond in ways that lead to feelings of comfort and even happiness, but unfairness causes our brains to respond with negative feelings such as anger and pain. The study found that this also happened when subjects saw other people being treated unfairly. They concluded that fairness is a basic human need along with food and social contact.

Our sense of fairness depends on the influences in our culture, the immediate situation we are in, and our own self-interest. Arriving at a feeling of fairness means considering different, often conflicting, points of view. Regardless of the disagreement, people almost always need to compromise. But it can be difficult to arrive at a compromise when there are conflicting interests. This is why communities have rules that everyone must follow.

Social controls are an important factor in setting and following rules. They influence the way we behave, and can be internal or external. Internal controls come from within and are based on our values and fears. Most of us don't steal, for example, because we believe that theft is unfair and wrong. We also don't want to disappoint our family and friends. In other words, our internal controls keep us from behaving in ways that cause conflict.

External controls include rewards and punishments. They do not come from within but are implemented by an authority—this could be the national or local government, the police, a manager, a teacher or parents, depending on the situation. Rewards,

such as job promotions, awards, and praise, are designed to encourage people to behave and act in the interest of the whole community. Punishments, such as public embarrassment, fines, and even imprisonment can prevent people from acting against the community's best interests, regardless of their values.

People need their communities to function smoothly. Because of this, humans most often behave in orderly, fair, and predictable ways. If there were no rules, the majority of people would probably continue to interact positively, like the subjects in the online avatar study. However, there would always be a minority who would not, with serious consequences. This is why a society without rules is unlikely to become a reality any time soon—at least not in the real world.

Developing critical thinking

Discuss these questions in a group.

1 If you could change the rules at your school or place of study, which rules would you change? Why?

I'd allow people to ...
I'd change the rule that says ...

2 Would you like to live in a community with no rules? Why or why not?

I'd like to live in a community with no rules. I think it would be ...
I wouldn't like to live in this kind of community because I'd be afraid some people would ...

ACADEMIC KEYWORDS		
encourage	(v)	/ɪnˈkʌrɪdʒ/
minority	(n)	/maɪˈnɔrəti/
respond	(v)	/rɪˈspɑnd/

READING 2 Ants: master collaborators

Before you read

Why do scientists study animals? What do you think people can learn from animals?

Global reading

Skim *Ants: master collaborators*. Where do you think the text comes from? Check (✓) its source.

☐ academic journal for researchers ☐ popular science magazine

☐ news section of the newspaper ☐ blog about current science news

THINK ABOUT

animal behavior and social order

how animals can inspire design

what animals can tell us about the environment

Close reading

NOTE TAKING: MAPPING

You can organize your notes with a map showing relationships between the main ideas. Skim the text and write down a phrase that summarizes each main idea. Leave room between each idea. Draw a box around each one. Then as you read more closely, add supporting details to your map. Write them around each main idea and draw boxes around them. Then draw lines to connect details to the main idea.

1 Read paragraphs 1 and 2 of *Ants: master collaborators* and complete the notes below.

work² _____ *for survival*

highly¹ _____ *societies*

Why we study ants

learn about³ _____ *and community*

each group has a⁴ _____ *job*

Eusocial insects (different roles)

roles—queens, ⁵ _____ *, and workers*

queens—largest—function is to⁶ _____

workers—look after⁸ _____ *and young, hunt, and⁹* _____ *the nest*

soldiers protect colony and find⁷ _____ *for nests*

2 Skim the rest of *Ants: master collaborators* and make maps using the main ideas below.

Similarities between ant and human communities

Differences between ant and human communities

3 Work in small groups. Compare your maps. Did you make similar maps? What are the differences?

Ants: master collaborators

Millions of ants live together in a colony, but they don't compete, get confused, or become disorganized. They behave in an amazingly orderly manner at all times. Some scientists refer to ants as "superorganisms" because they live in such highly organized societies that work together for survival. The way ants live and work together has made them one of the most important creatures on the planet. Scientists and researchers study ants to learn about collaboration and community.

Ants, like bees, belong to a class of eusocial insects. Eusocial insects are broken into groups within their community, and each group has a special job to do depending on the needs of the community. There are three basic groups in an ant colony: queens, soldiers, and workers. Queens are the largest ants, and their only job is to reproduce—they lay all of the eggs that will eventually become soldiers and workers. Soldiers are responsible for protecting the colony and finding new places for nests. Worker ants have many jobs within the community, including caring for the eggs and young ants, hunting for food and maintaining the nest.

The worker and soldier ants also divide into smaller groups. Each group has a job that complements the others. For example, one worker group extends the nest, and another repairs it. Others grow their own food like farmers, and still others manage small "farms" in which they raise smaller animals. In the same way as humans breed cows and use their milk, ants breed small insects called aphids and "milk" them to obtain a sugary liquid.

Some scientists are examining how studying ants can lead to a better understanding of labor issues, social class, and the use of natural resources in human communities. Ants have had millions of years of practice in working together to survive and grow. For a colony to function successfully, ants have to cooperate, and they do so without exception. Researchers hope that gathering information about how ants live together in communities can help people learn to cooperate and compromise with each other.

However, others argue that there are fundamental differences between ants and humans that mean human societies are unlikely ever to attain ant-like levels of collaboration. For example, ants in a colony don't compete with each other. When there is a shortage of food in the colony, some worker ants automatically become "feeder" ants and feed others with the food in their stomach, regardless of their usual job. When the food supply is replenished, they become worker ants again.

In addition, ants are able to work together without a leader giving them directions. Despite their name, queen ants are not leaders. Instead, ants find out what they need to do from their sense of smell. Research on harvester ants by Deborah Gordon and Michael Greene in 2010 showed that when harvester ants pass each other, they pick up a chemical smell which tells them what the other ant is doing. The number of ants they pass doing a particular job determines what they need to do. It is a form of communication, but unlike human communication it has no content; it is just based on numbers. If you are working in an office and you receive an email instructing you to do something, you know what to do because of the content of the email. If humans were like ants, it wouldn't matter what the email said—the important thing would be the number of emails.

While ants undoubtedly have a great deal to teach us about organization and the structure of networks, those searching for a greater understanding of human behavior and morals may need to look elsewhere.

Developing critical thinking

1 Discuss these questions in a group.

1 What would be the advantages and disadvantages if human communities were more like ant communities?

One advantage is that we would be more …
The biggest problem would be …

2 Some animals, like ants, are part of highly organized communities whereas others, like tigers, work only for themselves. Which do you think are more like humans? Why?

I think we are more like … because …

ACADEMIC KEYWORDS

attain	(v)	/əˈteɪn/
compete	(v)	/kəmˈpit/
structure	(n)	/ˈstrʌktʃər/

THINK ABOUT

| food | homes | jobs |
| rules | society | |

2 Think about the ideas from *Living by the rules* and *Ants: master collaborators* and discuss these questions in a group.

  1 What are the benefits of living with others in a community?

    One plus is ...
    An advantage could be ...

  2 What's difficult about being a member of a community?

    Living in a community is challenging because ...
    One thing that's difficult about it is ...

Vocabulary skill

SUFFIXES THAT CHANGE VERBS INTO NOUNS

Some verbs become nouns when we add a suffix, or ending, to them. Two common suffixes that perform this function are *-ion/-ation* and *-ment*.

verb	noun
confuse	confus**ion**
inform	inform**ation**
disagree	disagree**ment**

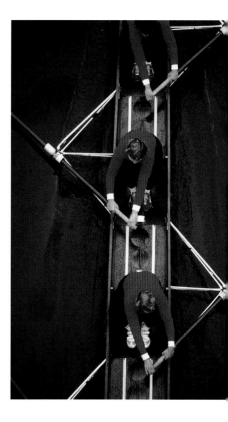

1 Add suffixes to change these verbs into nouns.

  1 promote   _____

  2 collaborate   _____

  3 confuse   _____

  4 inform   _____

  5 punish   _____

  6 embarrass   _____

  7 imprison   _____

  8 argue   _____

  9 disagree   _____

2 Circle the correct noun or verb form in these sentences.

  1 It's important to know how to **collaborate / collaboration** when working in a group.

  2 One **argue / argument** for community living is that it creates a supportive atmosphere.

  3 When there are set rules in place, people know what to expect and there is less **confuse / confusion**.

  4 It is unfair not to **punish / punishment** cheating.

  5 **Promote / Promotion** should be dependent on skills and experience, not who you know.

  6 The threat of **embarrass / embarrassment** is enough to discourage people from breaking rules.

  7 **Imprison / Imprisonment** is not an effective form of discipline.

  8 To be fair, every community has to **inform/ information** all of its members of the rules.

3 Work with a partner. Read the statements in exercise 2. Do you agree or disagree with them? Why?

WRITING Describing your community's rules

You are going to brainstorm ideas for writing with a chart and using verbs of obligation. You are then going to use these to write a paragraph describing rules in your community.

Writing skill

BRAINSTORMING: ORGANIZING YOUR IDEAS IN A CHART

After you brainstorm a list of ideas for writing, it's useful to make a chart to sort your ideas into categories. This will help you use a logical progression to write about your ideas.

Begin with main ideas. Scan your list and think of 2–4 categories your ideas fit into. From those categories start categorizing your ideas, adding categories as your chart grows. Look at the example below of a chart for an essay about rules.

How rules help us live in a community

Why we have rules	How rules are made	How rules influence behavior
people need fairness	cultural influence	social controls
keep people from cheating	self-interest	(internal—external)
...	interests of group as a whole	fear, embarrassment
	...	stricter punishments
		rewards
		...

Alternatively, you can think of some main points and then make a chart before you brainstorm. Then brainstorm ideas directly into your chart. There is no one correct way to make your chart.

1 Imagine you are going to write an essay describing the rules for a community you belong to. This could be your family, your college, a club or society you belong to, or even your city or country.

Choose three headings from the list below:
- How are the rules made?
- Why are there rules?
- What are the most important rules?
- What are the consequences of breaking the rules?

On a separate piece of paper, draw a chart and add your three headings.

2 **Brainstorm ideas directly into your chart, writing your ideas under the correct heading.**

3 **Compare charts with a partner. Are there ideas you didn't think of?**

Grammar

VERBS OF COMPULSION AND PROHIBITION

Verbs such as *make, stop, keep,* and *prevent* express compulsion and prohibition. We can also use *encourage, discourage,* and *expect,* which are not as strong.

Form	Example
<u>Make</u> + object + base form	What **makes** people follow rules?
<u>Stop, keep, prevent, and discourage</u> + object + *from* + verb + *-ing*	Social controls **stop** most people from breaking rules.
<u>Encourage and expect</u> + object + *to* + base form	We expect people **to follow** the rules.

1 Circle the correct form of the verbs.

   1 The fear of imprisonment can stop people **to steal** / **from stealing**.
   2 Rewards encourage individuals **behaving** / **to behave** in the interest of the larger group.
   3 Our internal controls can prevent us **breaking** / **from breaking** the law.
   4 Most people control themselves and expect others **do** / **to do** the same.
   5 The survival of the colony is what makes ants **cooperate** / **cooperating**.
   6 Most communities have rules that are designed to stop people **from acting** / **to act** in disorderly ways.

2 Complete the sentences with the correct form of the verbs. Use *to* or *from* if necessary.

   1 Internal controls keep people _____ (disobey) the rules in their community.
   2 Most people expect others _____ (behave) in ways that benefit the whole community.
   3 The fear of punishments such as imprisonment usually doesn't stop criminals _____ (break) the law.
   4 We can't make others _____ (follow) the rules; we can only choose to follow them ourselves.
   5 Rewards don't really encourage people _____ (cooperate) with each other.
   6 Rules in general prevent life _____ (become) too chaotic.

3 Work with a partner. Read the statements in exercise 2. Do you disagree with any of them? Why?

WRITING TASK

Write a short text describing rules you have in your community.

BRAINSTORM

1   Read the essay below and take notes into a mind map of the main ideas. Circle the verbs of compulsion and prohibition, as detailed on page 24.

Rules help us live together in a community. At my local park, there is a sign that reads, "Keep off the grass." Why do park officials want to stop people from walking on the grass?

Because our community has a need for a nice green space to relax, we are all expected to keep our park clean and in good condition for everyone's enjoyment. If everyone walked on the grass, the grass would die. No one would be able to enjoy a beautiful green park. Sometimes, people disobey the rules and play soccer on the grass. Although it's not enough to destroy the grass, I feel that everyone should obey the rules. If one person breaks the rules, then more people expect to be able to do what they want.

In a community, rules are in place to protect everyone. What we do and how we act affect everyone, not just ourselves. We need rules in order to live safely. If there were no rules or laws, it would be difficult to prevent people from committing more serious crimes.

2   You are going to write a 2–3-paragraph essay describing a special rule or rules in your community. Think about what it is, why it is in place, if it is valuable or not, if people always follow it, and if it is fair. Brainstorm a list of ideas and create a chart.

PLAN

Plan your essay. Look back at your brainstorm and decide how you want to organize your essay.

WRITE

Write an essay describing your community's rules. Pay attention to your use of verbs of compulsion and prohibition from page 24. Your essay should be 150–200 words long.

SHARE

Exchange paragraphs with a partner. Look at the checklist on page 109 and give feedback to your partner.

REWRITE AND EDIT

Read your partner's comments and edit your paragraph.

STUDY SKILLS Brainstorming and essay planning

Getting started

Discuss these questions with a partner.

1 When you are given an essay title, what do you do first?
2 What do you do when you haven't got any ideas?
3 What worries you most about essay writing?

Scenario

Read this scenario and think about what Khalid could have done instead.

Consider it

Read the tips about brainstorming and essay planning. Discuss each one with a partner. Why do you think it is important to do these things?

1 **Check it** It is very important to check you understand the essay title exactly. A small change in the essay title can mean a big change in what the teacher expects. Ask your tutor if you're not certain.
2 **Sum it up** Try to write one sentence that summarizes your main opinion or argument. This will help you to generate ideas.
3 **Brainstorm** Write down any ideas that come into your head. Don't worry if the ideas are strange or unusual. You don't have to use everything from the brainstorm in your final essay.
4 **Create an essay plan** Organize the ideas from your brainstorm. Use them to decide what the main sections of your essay are going to be, and then divide each section into paragraphs. Write a heading for each paragraph.
5 **Plan your research** Use your brainstorming and essay plan to help plan your research. Try to think about research questions. What do you need to know to be able to answer the question?
6 **Reflect** Once you have done your research, look at your main argument and essay plan again. Think about whether your opinion has changed, whether you have enough evidence for your arguments, and whether your essay plan still works. You may need to move, delete, or add paragraphs.

Over to you

Discuss these questions with a partner.

1 What is the advantage of brainstorming in groups?
2 Why is it important to research after brainstorming?
3 What should you do if you can't think of any ideas when brainstorming?

Khalid was given a difficult essay title, and he didn't know how to begin writing it. It was only 1,500 words and he had three weeks to write it, so he put it to one side for a week while he waited to find inspiration. When he looked at the title again, he still couldn't think of any ideas. He spent two hours staring at his computer and his class notes and came up with no ideas. The next night he just decided to try and write something. He wasn't sure he understood the question, so he picked out the key words in the title and just focused on those. He wrote down everything he knew on that topic as soon as it came into his head, as he found he could write faster that way. When he had written almost 1,500 words, he stopped and wrote two sentences as a conclusion. He then checked his spelling and grammar and handed it in. He knew it wasn't his best essay, but he thought it was OK. He was surprised to receive a "fail" grade.

Space

READING	Identifying definitions
	Creating a text plan
VOCABULARY	Scientific terms with Latin and Greek roots
WRITING	Using a variety of sentence types
GRAMMAR	Passive voice

Discussion point

Discuss these questions with a partner.

1 What do you think fascinates people about space?

People are fascinated by space because ...

2 Why is it important to study our universe?

It's important to study our universe because ...

3 Some people think that space exploration is a waste of money and we should focus on solving problems on Earth. What's your opinion?

I think space exploration is/isn't a waste of money because ...
It would be better to spend the money on ...

Vocabulary preview

Use the words from the box to complete the text.

chance	estimates	interpret	odds	predicted
scenario	simulate	speculate		

Many books and movies (1) _____ about the possibility of life
on other planets. Some scientists believe there's a good (2) _____
that there is life on another planet somewhere. For example, Gerrard has
(3) _____ that we will discover extraterrestrial life within the
next 50 years. However, others such as Watson believe it's less likely. She
(4) _____ that the (5) _____ are around 1 in 100,000.
Some people even claim to have been abducted by extraterrestrials. However,
scientists believe this is due to a condition called sleep paralysis, which can
cause the mind to (6) _____ an unreal (7) _____ such as
alien abduction and (8) _____ it as reality.

READING 1 Discovered by amateurs

Before you read

Discuss with a partner.

Why do you think astronomy is a popular hobby and science?

It's popular because ...

Global reading

Skim *Discovered by amateurs* and check (✓) what it is about.

- [ ] NASA scientists' discoveries in space
- [ ] a new organization for people who are interested in space
- [ ] space discoveries made by non-professionals
- [ ] how to become an astronaut

Close reading

IDENTIFYING DEFINITIONS

When you read a factual article, look for definitions of topic-specific vocabulary you are
not familiar with. A signal can be a word or phrase, such as *or*, *in other words*, or *that is*,
or punctuation, such as a comma, parentheses, or dashes.

Kathryn had found a supernova, **or an exploding star**.

*The star becomes brighter than the rest of its galaxy—**a huge system of stars and gases**.*

**Scan *Discovered by amateurs* for signals that point to definitions within the text. Then
complete the sentences with definitions of the words in bold.**

1 A **supernova**— *an exploding star* —is brighter than its galaxy.

2 A **galaxy** is defined as _____.

3 Kathryn is an **amateur astronomer**; in other words, she is _____.

4 Uranus was eventually identified as a **planet**, that is, _____.

5 Today Pluto is classified as a **dwarf** (_____) planet.

Supernova 2010lt

Galaxy UGC 3378

DISCOVERED BY AMATEURS

1 Some astronomers spend their entire careers looking for new discoveries in space, but a ten-year-old Canadian girl found one on her first try. In January 2011, Kathryn Gray was looking at recent pictures of outer space and comparing them to pictures taken years earlier. The pictures were just thousands of tiny spots of light, but Kathryn spotted a star that looked different in the recent pictures. She knew a lot about space and was excited by what she thought she'd found—could it possibly be a supernova?

2 Supernovas, or exploding stars, are a huge event in space. When a star dies, an enormous amount of energy is released. So much light and radiation is emitted by a supernova that the star becomes brighter than the rest of its galaxy—an enormous system of stars and gases. Due to their brightness, supernovas become visible through telescopes. However, it's not easy to find supernovas, nor are they common. The European Space Agency estimates that in a galaxy the size of the Milky Way, a supernova happens about once every 50 years.

3 Kathryn immediately went to show her discovery to her father. He too is an amateur astronomer—he is very interested in space, but he isn't formally trained in astronomy—so he sent the pictures to a lab, where they were examined by experts. The discovery was confirmed the next day, and Kathryn became the youngest person ever to discover a supernova.

4 Throughout history, important discoveries in astronomy have been made by amateurs. An early example is William Herschel, a musician whose hobby was astronomy. Herschel discovered Uranus in 1781. Uranus had been observed before, but expert astronomers thought it was a star, not part of our own solar system (a collection of planets and their sun). When Herschel saw it with a telescope he had designed and built himself, he realized that it was orbiting (moving around) the sun. This meant that Uranus could be classified as a planet. And so, the map of our night sky was changed forever.

5 Then in 1930, a major discovery was made by a 24-year old farmer's son with no college education or formal training in astronomy. In 1928, Clyde Tombaugh had built a homemade telescope using instructions from an article in a boy's magazine which he used to draw detailed pictures of the surfaces of Mars and Jupiter. He sent the pictures to Dr. V. M. Slipher at the Lowell Observatory who was so impressed he offered him a job on his team. Within a year, Tombaugh had discovered a ninth planet, Pluto. It was regarded as a planet for 76 years, but scientists decided in 2006 that Pluto didn't meet all of the criteria for a true planet. It was then classified as a dwarf, or small, planet.

6 John Dobson is considered to be one of the most influential amateur astronomers because he enabled so many others to take up astronomy as a hobby. In 1956, he built a powerful telescope out of low-cost materials, such as paper tubes used in construction. With affordable tools like Dobson's telescope, more amateurs today have the technology that is needed to make significant discoveries of their own.

ACADEMIC KEYWORDS

classify	(v)	/ˈklæsɪˌfaɪ/
influential	(adj)	/ˌɪnfluˈenʃəl/
within	(prep)	/wɪðˈɪn/

Developing critical thinking

Discuss these questions in a group.

1 Which of the amateurs' discoveries mentioned in the text was the most significant achievement, in your opinion? Why?

I think ...'s discovery was very important because ...
The discovery of ... was a big achievement because ...

2 Do you think outer space is important to us here on Earth? Why or why not?

Events in space affect us because ...
Whatever happens in space has very little effect on Earth because ...

THINK ABOUT
a waste of money/time
climate change
conduct experiments
investigate
monitor pollution
priority

READING 2 Close encounters

Before you read

1 **Look at the events in the box. Which do you think is most likely to happen in the next 50 years?**

... is the most/least likely to happen because ...

2 **What do you think would happen if a large object like a meteor collided with Earth?**

It's likely that ...

Global reading

CREATING A TEXT PLAN

Creating a text plan as you read can make it much easier to navigate a text. When you skim read, you are looking for the general meaning of the whole text and of individual paragraphs. To create a text plan, note the general meaning of each paragraph the first time you read, and then decide which paragraphs can be grouped together.

Read *Close encounters*. Then complete the plan of the text with the words in the box.

collisions	comet	Earth	Examples (×2)	Introduction	Jupiter
measuring	Near Earth Objects	Odds	pattern	risk	soon

Para1 Setting scene—(1) _____ hit by comet, could similar collision happen on (2) _____ ?

Para2 Examples of (3) _____ strikes

Para3 (4) _____ of asteroid strikes

Para4 Number of (5) _____

Para5 (6) _____ of large collision in our lifetime

Para6 Techniques for (7) _____ (8) _____ of collisions

Para7 (9) _____ to collisions—next one (10) _____ ?

(11) _____

(12) _____ of previous (13) _____

Possibility of future collisions

Close reading

Read each sentence from *Close encounters*. Write *M* (main idea) or *D* (detail).

1 It is estimated that one comet passes between Earth and the moon every 100 years, and one strikes the Earth about every 100,000 years. ____

2 These scenarios are possible, yet most people don't change their lifestyle to avoid these minimal risks. ____

3 Scientists have developed techniques for measuring the risk of such events. ____

4 An NEO larger than 6 km., which could cause mass extinction, will collide with Earth every hundred million years. ____

CLOSE ENCOUNTERS

HOME • BLOG • STORIES • MESSAGE BOARD

1 In 1993, a vast object orbiting Jupiter was discovered by an amateur observer and two other astronomers. About a year later, that comet—an object in space made of ice and dust—struck Jupiter. The impact on Jupiter was visible from Earth for many months afterwards, and the outer edge of the damage was the size of the Earth in diameter. One of the first people to observe the comet, Eugene Shoemaker, said that if a similar comet hit Earth, it would be catastrophic: "… we're talking about a million megatons of kinetic energy. We're talking about the kind of event that is associated with mass extinction of species on Earth; really and truly a global catastrophe." Could something this big strike Earth, and if so, would it be as bad as Shoemaker claims?

2 Comets do not pass near to the Earth frequently, and fortunately they strike even less often. It is estimated that one comet passes between Earth and the moon every 100 years, and one strikes Earth about every 100,000 years. It is believed that one of these impacts caused such destruction that it was responsible for the mass extinction of the dinosaurs. Closer to the present day, the largest recorded impact in recent history was in Siberia in 1909. The impact of this comet is thought to have destroyed 80 million trees covering 2,150 square kilometers. Had the explosion happened over a city, it could have devastated a large metropolitan area.

3 Another space object that passes Earth more frequently is an asteroid. In 2011, a small asteroid (a rocky body that orbits the sun) passed very close to Earth only two days after it was discovered. Its distance from Earth—around 180,000 km., roughly half the distance of the Earth to the moon—worried some, but astronomers assured people that an asteroid would burn up in the atmosphere before striking Earth.

4 So do we have any idea of how many of these objects might be near Earth right now? Astronomers use sophisticated computers and electronic imaging to scan the skies for potentially dangerous asteroids and comets. To date NASA has identified almost 9,000 Near Earth Objects (asteroids and comets) over 1 km. wide—in other words, large enough to cause regional devastation.

5 While this sounds alarming, the chance that Earth will be hit by something large enough to cause worldwide damage during our lifetime is about 1 in 10,000. Those are the same odds of dying in a car accident during any six-month period, or of dying of cancer from breathing polluted air every day. These scenarios are possible, yet most people don't change their lifestyle to avoid these minimal risks.

6 Scientists have developed techniques for measuring the risk of such events. One scale used to measure the likelihood of such an event is the Torino scale. This scale gives a score between 0 and 10, with 10 an almost certain hit. So far no object has ever rated above 4, which indicates a mere 1% chance of causing regional devastation.

7 However, some believe that major collisions in the past show a pattern which suggests the next one may come soon. Monica Grady, an expert in meteorites at the Open University, says: "It's a question of when, not if, a Near Earth Object collides with Earth. Many of the smaller objects break up when they reach the Earth's atmosphere and have no impact. However, an NEO larger than 1 km. (in width) will collide with Earth every few hundred thousand years, and an NEO larger than 6 km., which could cause mass extinction, will collide with Earth every hundred million years." Many scientists believe that if such events follow a regular pattern, we can expect another one at any time. "We are overdue for a big one," Grady says.

ACADEMIC KEYWORDS

likelihood	(n)	/ˈlaɪkliˌhʊd/
potentially	(adv)	/pəˈtenʃəli/
scale	(n)	/skeɪl/

Developing critical thinking

1 Discuss these questions in a group.

1 What do you think would happen if scientists predicted that a large object from space was likely to strike Earth?

I think some people might …
I think governments would …

2 Is it worth spending millions of dollars predicting when space collisions might occur, or should this money be spent on other things, like finding cures for diseases?

2 **Think about the ideas from *Discovered by amateurs* and *Close encounters* and discuss these questions in a group.**

1 If amateurs can make discoveries about space before the experts, how confident can we be about expert astronomers and their predictions regarding space collisions?

We can be very confident because ...
We shouldn't trust their predictions because ...

2 We know more about space than we do about the seas and oceans on Earth. Why do you think so much attention has been focused on the universe beyond Earth? Think about the ideas in the box.

THINK ABOUT

attitudes of countries and governments towards space exploration and research

financial support for space exploration

why people are interested in space

why we need to know more about space

Vocabulary skill

SCIENTIFIC TERMS WITH LATIN AND GREEK ROOTS

Many scientific terms in English come from Latin and Greek roots. Understanding roots can help you understand the meaning of a word. For example:

The root **astro** means "star." The word *astronomy* means the scientific study of stars.

The root **sol** means "sun." The *solar* system is everything connected to one sun/star.

The root **bio** means "life." *Biology* is the study of life.

1 **Read the example sentences and match the roots with the meanings in the box.**

| light | ~~earth~~ | breathing | stars | heat | mind |

1 I enjoyed physical ***geo*graphy** at school, especially studying earthquakes and volcanoes.

geo = earth

2 Many people practice ***astro*nomy** as a hobby because they are interested in the universe.

3 A ***thermo*meter** was used to measure change in temperature.

4 Without spacesuits, ***respir*ation** is impossible in space.

5 It is not uncommon for people who believe they have been abducted by aliens to see a ***psych*iatrist**.

6 Plants create their own food through a process known as ***photo*synthesis** where they gain energy from the sun.

2 **Complete these sentences with the words in the box.**

| astronomer | geology | photographs |
| psychology | respirator | thermodynamics |

1 _____ is the study of the relationship between heat and energy.

2 _____ is the study of the Earth, the rocks it is made of, and how they have changed over time.

3 An _____ studies the stars.

4 _____ are made using a process involving light.

5 Sometimes sick people need a _____ to help them breathe.

6 _____ is the study of the mind.

WRITING Describing an amateur discovery

You are going to learn reasons why writers sometimes use the passive voice. You are also going to learn how to use different techniques to add variety to your sentences. Then you are going to write a paragraph about a discovery made by an amateur.

Grammar

PASSIVE VOICE

The passive voice is frequently found in academic texts and factual articles. Authors choose to use the passive voice when they want to focus on the action itself and not the person or people doing the action. This can be because the person doing the action is unknown or unimportant.

*The pictures **had been taken** on a recent New Year's Eve. (who took the pictures is unknown and/or unimportant)*

By is used in the passive to indicate the person doing the action while keeping the focus on the action itself.

*In 1993, an object orbiting Jupiter was discovered **by** an amateur observer and two other astronomers.*

1   **Find these examples of the passive in *Discovered by amateurs* and *Close encounters*. With a partner, decide why the author chose to use the passive in each case.**

   1   He sent the pictures to a lab, where they were examined by experts.
   2   Throughout history, important discoveries in astronomy have been made by amateurs.
   3   It is estimated that one comet passes between Earth and the moon every 100 years, and one strikes Earth about every 100,000 years.
   4   The chance that Earth will be hit by something large enough to cause worldwide damage is about 1 in 10,000.
   5   It was regarded as a planet for 76 years.

2   **Circle the active or passive form of the verb to complete these sentences.**

   1   The discovery **confirmed / was confirmed** the next day.
   2   Uranus **had observed / had been observed** already, but astronomers thought it was a star.
   3   Experts **define / are defined** a planet as a round body that orbits the sun.
   4   An asteroid passed close to Earth two days after it **discovered / was discovered**.
   5   A huge asteroid **struck / was struck** Earth early in its life as a planet.
   6   Earth **struck / was struck** by an unknown object early in its history.

3   **Change these sentences from the active to passive form.**

   1   Many people often confuse science fiction with science fact.
   2   Scientists will analyze the results.
   3   People use a barometer for measuring atmospheric pressure.
   4   Some people think another strike on Earth will happen soon.

Writing skill

USING A VARIETY OF SENTENCE TYPES

Good writers use a variety of sentence types to make their writing more interesting. One way is to combine simple sentences using the conjunctions *and, but, nor, yet,* and *so*.

The pictures were just thousands of tiny spots of light.

Kathryn spotted a star that looked different.

*The pictures were just thousands of tiny spots of light, **but** Kathryn spotted a star that looked different.*

It's not easy to find supernovas.

Supernovas are not common.

*It's not easy to find supernovas, **nor** are they common.*

Another approach is to use a variety of subjects for sentences in the same paragraph. You can change the subject while keeping the same meaning.

***Comets** are objects in space made of ice and dust.*

*Ice and dust combine in space to form **comets**.*

1 **Compare the sentences on the left and the paragraph on the right. Then match the numbered sections (1–5 in the paragraph) with the technique the author has used to vary the sentence type (a–d).**

Comets are objects in space made of ice and dust. Comets do not pass near Earth frequently. Comets strike Earth even less regularly than they pass near it. Comets are estimated to pass between Earth and the moon once every 100 years. Comets strike Earth about once every 100,000 years.

[1]Ice and dust combine in space to form comets. [2]These bright extraterrestrial objects do not pass near to the Earth frequently, [3]and fortunately they strike even less regularly. [4]It is estimated that one comet passes between Earth and the moon every 100 years, [5]and one strikes Earth about every 100,000 years.

a   change from active to passive *4*

b   replace the subject with a synonym or descriptive phrase ....

c   change from passive to active ....

d   add a conjunction ....

2 **Rewrite these sentences using a variety of sentence types.**

1   A comet struck Jupiter in 1993. (change from active to passive)

_____

2   The galaxy we live in is called the Milky Way. (replace subject with a descriptive phrase)

_____

3   A major discovery was made by a 24-year-old farmer's son. (change from passive to active)

_____

4   These scenarios are possible. Most people don't change their lifestyle to avoid these minimal risks. (add a conjunction)

_____

WRITING TASK

Write an article about an amateur discovery.

BRAINSTORM

1 Read the paragraph. Circle the conjunctions and underline verbs in the passive voice.

The record for discovering the most supernovas is held by Robert Evans, an amateur astronomer from Australia. His skill at noticing changes in the sky is remarkable; it has been described as being able to spot a grain of salt that has been added to a table covered in salt. Evans doesn't generally have access to an observatory, nor does he use fancy equipment. Most professional astronomers use huge, high-tech telescopes to watch the sky, yet Evans's record was achieved with much smaller amateur's telescopes. In 1983, Evans discovered a previously unknown type of supernova, so in addition to discovering 42 supernovas to date, he has also contributed to our knowledge of them.

2 Think about a real or imaginary discovery made by an amateur. Write notes on who discovered it, how they discovered it, what's important about the discovery, and any other important details.

PLAN

Plan your article. Look at your brainstormed list and write a topic sentence. You may want to tell an interesting story to draw in the reader before you introduce the topic.

WRITE

Write a two to three paragraph article describing an exciting discovery. Pay attention to your use of the passive voice. Vary your sentence structure and the conjunctions you use. Your article should be 150–200 words long.

SHARE

Exchange articles with a partner. Read the checklist on page 109 and provide feedback to your partner.

REWRITE AND EDIT

Consider your partner's comments and write a final draft of your article.

Improving reading comprehension

by Stella Cottrell

Do I understand what I read?

Do you:

- [ ] understand most of what you read?
- [ ] know how much you understand?
- [ ] understand uninteresting material?
- [ ] actively monitor your understanding?
- [ ] know how to improve comprehension?

If you answered "no" to one or more of these questions, experiment with the following active reading strategies to improve your comprehension.

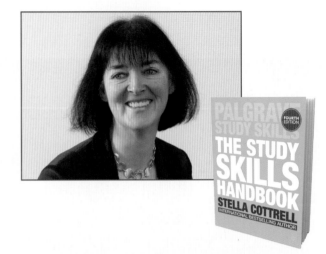

Active reading strategies

Start with something general

Reading is easier if you have a sense of the context and a general overview. Read the most basic text you can find first. Familiarize yourself with the main issues and the vocabulary.

Monitor your comprehension

Read a few sentences, then stop. Without looking back at the text, sum up what you have read in just a few words. Say these words aloud, or jot them down. If you cannot do this, read back over what you have read, using an additional strategy from below.

Guide your reading

Set yourself specific questions to start off your reading. Write them down. Adapt the questions as your reading progresses. The clearer you are about what you are trying to discover, the easier it is to find it in the text.

Re-read difficult passages

Academic texts often contain difficult passages. Don't panic! It's normal to need to re-read some passages slowly, several times.

Highlight key words and phrases

On your own text or a photocopy, underline in pencil the information you think may be relevant.

Look especially at headings, and first and last sentences of paragraphs. Select a few of the key words you underlined and highlight them in color. Double-underline or star very important points. Make a faint wavy line at the side of fairly important passages. Be selective! If you underline or highlight everything, *nothing* will stand out as important.

Color-code information

Use different colors for different kinds of information—for example, one color for reference names and dates, and one for each of the main schools of thought or major theories for the subject. Later, just seeing that color combination on the page may remind you what the page was about.

Ask "depth questions"

Look for the underlying issues:

- What point is the writer making?
- Why is this detail relevant?
- Is the writer trying to answer a particular question?
- What lessons can be learned from this text?

Relaxed reading

Reading comprehension is improved when the body is relaxed. Use appropriate lighting; have music or silence, as you prefer; and drink plain water.

How do I approach reading tasks now?

How could I spend my reading time more effectively?

Scale

READING	Summarizing
	Pronoun referents
VOCABULARY	Comparing and contrasting
WRITING	Complex sentences
GRAMMAR	Comparatives and superlatives

Discussion point

Discuss these questions with a partner.

1 Look at the picture. How would you describe this building? Where do you think it is?

   It looks really ...

2 What are some of the biggest buildings in your country? Do you know what's in the buildings?

   The tallest building is located in ...
   It's used for ...

3 What are the advantages and disadvantages for consumers of buying from large companies?

Vocabulary preview

Complete the sentences with the words in the box.

> behavior   consumers   debt   demand   generation   satisfaction

1 In the past, _____ went to several small stores to buy groceries.
2 E-commerce has affected consumer _____, allowing specialized
   stores to take market share in a global marketplace.
3 Online presence means that a small business can meet consumer _____ overseas.
4 A change of attitude toward _____ means more people borrow money from the bank.
5 Our grandparents' _____ did not have easy access to credit cards.
6 Consumers want instant _____; if they want it, they buy it.

READING 1   The superconsumer generation

Before you read

Discuss these questions with a partner.

1 Where do you shop most often? Do you ever shop online?

   I normally shop in ...   I buy / don't buy ... online ...

2 What was the last thing you bought from a shop?

Global reading

> **SUMMARIZING**
>
> Summarizing is giving a brief statement of the most important points of a
> text. As you read, highlight or underline the main points of the text. Then
> use the information to write a summary. Even when you are just writing a
> summary for your notes, you should use your own words to avoid potentially
> plagiarizing the text if you decide to use it in an assignment later.

1 **Read *The superconsumer generation*. Look at the summary of the first half
   of the text. What is good about it? What would you change?**

> Shopping malls have grown dramatically in size to satisfy today's consumer
> demands, in particular those of Generation Y, people born in the late
> seventies to early eighties. Worldwide, Gen Y-ers are showing more and
> more similarities in their consumer behavior. Where previous generations
> bought from locally owned businesses, Gen Y shop at large multinational
> retailers such as Walmart, which has 8,500 stores in 15 different countries.

2 **Read *The superconsumer generation* again and complete the second half
   of the summary using the words in the box.**

> choice   debt   decade   demanding   explosion
> loyalty   online   understand

Generation Y has a huge (1) _____ of products, especially when they shop (2) _____.
Due to the (3) _____ in online shopping over the last (4) _____, it has become a normal
way to shop for Gen-Y. Large companies want to target Gen Y-ers because they spend a lot and they do not
worry about (5) _____. However, they are also very (6) _____. Companies need to
(7) _____ them if they want to gain their (8) _____.

THE

Close reading

Read *The superconsumer generation* again. Mark each sentence *T* (true), *F* (false), or *NG* (not given).

1 Almost as many people go to the Dubai Mall every week as live in Dubai. _____
2 Gen Y-ers were all born in the 1970s. _____
3 Walmart has a bigger income than many countries in the world. _____
4 People spend more on the internet than in stores. _____
5 Generation Y-ers have grown up with credit cards _____
6 Gen Y-ers are not important consumers. _____
7 Technology can help keep Generation Y loyal. _____

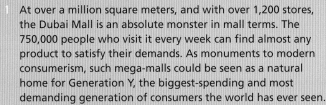
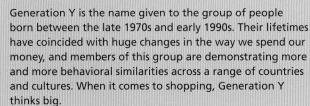

1 At over a million square meters, and with over 1,200 stores, the Dubai Mall is an absolute monster in mall terms. The 750,000 people who visit it every week can find almost any product to satisfy their demands. As monuments to modern consumerism, such mega-malls could be seen as a natural home for Generation Y, the biggest-spending and most demanding generation of consumers the world has ever seen.

2 Generation Y is the name given to the group of people born between the late 1970s and early 1990s. Their lifetimes have coincided with huge changes in the way we spend our money, and members of this group are demonstrating more and more behavioral similarities across a range of countries and cultures. When it comes to shopping, Generation Y thinks big.

3 While their parents' generation may well have known many store owners personally, members of Generation Y are more likely to buy from huge multinational companies like Walmart which has 8,500 stores in 15 different countries. In 2011, Walmart made sales of over 400 billion U.S. dollars, which is bigger than the GDP of 150 countries worldwide.

4 While consumers of the Generation Y era can choose from a huge range of products at giant shopping malls, they have even more choice online. Gen Y-ers, as they are known, have grown up with the Internet, and using technology in all areas of their lives is second nature to them. In just over a decade, internet shopping has seen an explosion in growth. In the U.K., for example, consumers spent just £800 million online in 2000; by 2010 this had grown to almost £60 billion. Amazon, the world's largest online retailer, sells such a wide variety of products they have to be stored in huge warehouses the size of ten soccer fields.

5 Gen Y-ers are prime targets for retail companies because of their spending power and attitude to shopping. In the U.S. alone, their purchasing power as a group stands at $108 billion. And if they don't have enough money to buy what they want, they turn to their good friend, the credit card. Credit cards became a global phenomenon in the 1990s, so they are a normal part of life for Generation Y. In the past, many people viewed getting into debt as something negative, but now using credit cards is common. Rather than saving to buy, today's younger generation happily uses credit to gain instant gratification.

6 Gen Y-ers though, unfortunately for companies, are considered the toughest group yet to satisfy. One of the biggest challenges facing companies is the fact that Gen Y-ers do not want to be labeled or put together into one group. They want products and services to be adapted to meet their needs as individuals. The group is wary of any attempt to influence them and unlikely to believe any advertising message. And they expect any problems to be solved instantly.

7 The older and wealthier Gen Y consumers become, the more important it is for companies to understand them. If a company can use technology to personalize its products and services, it might just gain the loyalty of the least loyal consumers in history.

SUPERCONSUMER GENERATION

Developing critical thinking

Discuss these questions in a group.

1 Think of your parents' and grandparents' generations. Are they different from you in the way they shop? Why do you think older generations are often slower to accept technological changes?

2 Do you think the change in retailing is positive or negative? Think of at least two positives and two negatives.

ACADEMIC KEYWORDS

absolute	(adj)	/ˈæbsəˌlut/
coincide	(v)	/ˌkoʊɪnˈsaɪd/
range	(n)	/reɪndʒ/

READING 2 The sky's the limit

Before you read

1 Think about how a city in your country has changed during your lifetime. Work with a partner. Make notes on the topics in the *Think about* box.

2 Share your ideas with another pair.

Global reading

Skim *The sky's the limit*. Then match the headings with the paragraphs.

1	Why are tall buildings built?	paragraph ___
2	The financial impact of tall structures	paragraph ___
3	The history of tall buildings	paragraph ___
4	The future	paragraph ___
5	An example of a controversial tall building	paragraph ___
6	Tallest skyscrapers of the last hundred years	paragraph ___

Close reading

PRONOUN REFERENTS

Pronouns are used instead of repeating the same word many times. They commonly refer backward to a name or idea, but they can also refer forward. It is important to understand which idea the pronoun refers to in order to fully understand the text. These are some of the most commonly used pronouns:

<u>People</u>

he, she, we, you, they, who, them, my, your, her, his, our, their, me, him, her, his, our

<u>Objects and ideas</u>

it, this, these, those, that, there, its

1 **Look at paragraph 2 of *The sky's the limit*. Find each of these pronouns and decide what each refers to.**

> it   these   this

2 **Read *The sky's the limit*. Find these pronouns. What does each refer to?**

1 it (paragraph 4)   = _____
2 its (paragraph 5) = _____
3 its (paragraph 6) = _____
4 it (paragraph 6)   = _____
5 that (paragraph 6) = _____

THE SKY'S THE LIMIT

1 **For centuries,** some of the tallest buildings in the world were religious buildings, but few were ever more than 150 meters tall. Almost all of these buildings took decades or even hundreds of years to complete. However, the invention of steel frames in the late 1800s meant that the walls did not carry the weight of a structure. This development meant that suddenly much taller buildings were possible, and they could be built quickly. Skyscrapers had been born, and they were about to change the the face of our cities.

2 **Since 1901,** the world's tallest building has always been a skyscraper, and until 1974 this was always in New York. The most famous of these was the Empire State Building. It held the record as the world's tallest building for over 40 years, longer than any building in modern history. Only after the end of the century did the tallest building appear outside North America, with the opening in Taipei of the first building to be more than half a kilometer tall, Taipei 101. However, all of these were to be dwarfed by the opening of the Burj Khalifa in Dubai in 2010, which showed an incredible 62% increase in height on the previous world's tallest building. Most new record holders had only ever shown an increase of between 5% and 20%.

3 **Countries and cities** have been competing with each other for centuries to hold records for the tallest structures. To many people tall buildings are a sign of modernity, wealth, power, and success. The Eiffel Tower, once the tallest structure in the world, was built as part of the 1889 World's Fair to celebrate the hundredth anniversary of the French Revolution, and to highlight France's design and engineering skill. For centuries, the contest to build the world's tallest structures was dominated by Europe and then North America, but today the economic growth and power of countries in other regions has seen a dramatic shift in the location of "supertall" building construction.

4 **Tall buildings** are seen as a symbol of success and status by many, but they are not always popular with local residents, particularly in some historic cities. London is very old and is spread over a vast area, so there are not many tall buildings in the center of the city. As a result, the construction of the Shard, the tallest building in London and in the entire European Union, has been highly controversial. It is only a few hundred meters across the River Thames from the Tower of London—one of the oldest and most famous landmarks in London. Many feel that such modern constructions should not be built near to historic sites.

5 **Not surprisingly,** considering the levels of debt in the U.K. at the time of construction, the Shard has largely been funded by external investment. The vast majority of funds have been provided by a Qatari investment fund. However, London residents should hope that its opening doesn't lead to a major downturn in their economy. The Empire State Building was finished in 1931, very soon after Wall Street crashed. The Petronas Towers in Kuala Lumpur were built in 1998, just after the Asian financial crisis. The Taipei 101 in Taiwan, constructed between 1999 and 2003, was closely linked to the dotcom bubble. The Burj Khalifa in Dubai was opened in early 2010, and shortly afterwards the emirate's investment company collapsed.

6 **The Burj Khalifa** might be the tallest structure in the world currently, but its status is under threat from numerous planned buildings around the world. Two likely future contenders for the title are the Burj Mubarak Al Kabir in Kuwait and the Kingdom Tower in Saudi Arabia, both of which would be over 1,000 m. if constructed as planned. One tower which will probably never be built is the 4 km. high X-Seed 4000 in Tokyo, which would house over a million people across 800 floors. It was designed in 1995 to attract publicity rather than as a serious proposal, but who knows when such fanciful ideas could become a reality? The Burj Khalifa is more than double the height of the Empire State Building, and surely no one in 1931 would have imagined that.

Developing critical thinking

1 **Discuss these questions in a group.**

1 Why do you think some countries and cities see modern developments as positive and others see them as negative?

2 Why do you think the construction of large buildings is often closely linked to financial disasters?

I think one of the reasons could be that ...

SCALE **UNIT 4** 41

2 Think about the ideas from *The superconsumer generation* and *The sky's the limit* and discuss these questions in a group.

1 Organizations get into debt building skyscrapers while today's consumers get into debt spending too much on their credit cards. Why do you think this happens? Are the reasons the same in both cases?

2 In many cities, the largest buildings are shopping malls. Do you think this will change as internet shopping grows? Why or why not?

Vocabulary skill

FOR COMPARING AND CONTRASTING

Certain vocabulary is used to make comparisons or contrasts. Noticing and understanding the meaning and function of words for describing similarities and differences can help you understand the organization of a text and help your overall understanding.

1 Look at the words in *italics* in the following sentences and decide if they describe similarities or differences. Write *S* or *D*.

1 Paper book sales have fallen, *while* e-book sales have grown. ___

2 *Unlike* a small retailer, a big department store often has a wide range of products. ___

3 Almost *as* many people live in urban areas in China *as* live in rural parts. ___

4 *The distinction between* government debt and much private debt is that governments usually have the resources to pay these off. ___

5 In the past, cities tended to grow outward. *Conversely*, today they tend to grow upward. ___

6 One of the most famous old buildings in London, Harrods, is now owned by Qatari investors. *Likewise*, the newest London landmark is also Qatari-owned. ___

7 Construction of large towers is often seen as a show of wealth. *On the other hand*, it can signal the start of a decline. ___

2 (Circle) the best words to complete these sentences.

1 Older people tend to buy CDs in stores. _____, teenagers tend to download music.
   a Conversely   **b** Likewise   **c** The distinction between

2 _____ two generations is often shown through music, fashion, and business.
   a Similarly   **b** On the other hand   **c** The difference between

3 _____ previous generations, who would save to buy a product, many people today use debt to buy what they want.
   a Likewise   **b** Unlike   **c** Conversely,

4 _____ previous generations, customers now have more product choice but less choice of retailers.
   a Compared with   **b** Conversely   **c** Likewise,

5 Many people want a greater choice of food products all year round. _____ some prefer to buy seasonal and local produce.
   a On the other hand,   **b** Unlike   **c** Likewise,

6 The largest bookstore in Europe holds over 150,000 books, _____ Amazon stocks millions of titles.
   a similarly,   **b** the distinction between   **c** while

WRITING Comparing consumer behavior

You are going to learn about complex sentences, and using comparative and superlative structures. You are then going to use these to write a paragraph comparing people from different generations.

Writing skill

COMPLEX SENTENCES

A complex sentence has two or more clauses. Unlike a compound sentence, where the two clauses are independent, a complex sentence always has a dependent clause. A dependent clause has a subject and a verb, but cannot stand alone in a sentence. For example:

dependent clause	independent clause
If a company can use its technology to do this,	*it might make the least loyal consumers stay with them.*

dependent clause	independent clause
While London is one of the most populous cities,	*it is not even in the top 50 for density.*

Subordinating conjunctions are used to start a dependent clause. Common subordinating conjunctions include:

Time: *after, before, while, since*   Reason: *as, because, so that, since,*

But: *although*   Possible situation: *if*   Alternative/contrast: *while*

---

1 Read the paragraph and ⟨circle⟩ the correct subordinating conjunction.

[1]**Before / While** the introduction of the Internet most people purchased their books in stores. Although the appearance of ebook readers such as the Amazon Kindle has had a major effect on bookstores, the decline in store sales began much earlier. [2]**Before / Since** the beginning of online retail and the launch of ebook readers, many small bookstores have closed down. [3]**While / Since** the Kindle is not the only ebook reader, it has certainly played a major role in the ebook revolution. [4]**Since / When** the launch of the first Kindle in 2007, ebook sales have grown dramatically every year. It would be surprising [5]**if / because** the local bookstore survived another decade.

2 Complete the sentences with the subordinating conjunctions in the box.

although	because	if	when	while

1 _____ I have CDs, I mostly download music nowadays.

2 _____ I go to the mall, I like to spend time shopping with my friends and having lots of coffee breaks.

3 My generation is different from previous generations _____ we all like to be treated individually.

4 _____ shopping online, I also check out Facebook.

5 My parents only shop online _____ they think the site is safe.

3 Discuss with a partner which sentences in exercise 2 are true for you.

Grammar

COMPARATIVES AND SUPERLATIVES

The comparative form uses *-er* or *more* with the adjective. The superlative form uses *most* or *-est* and the adjective. Note *the* is used with the superlative form

Form	Example
<u>One syllable adjectives</u> Add *-er*, *-est*, or *the -est*. If the adjective ends in vowel + consonant, double the final consonant.	*low lower lowest* *fast faster fastest* *big bigger biggest* *hot hotter hottest*
<u>Two syllable adjectives</u> If the adjective ends in *-y*, change the *y* to *i* and add *-er* or *-est*. If the adjective doesn't end in *-y*, add *more* or *the most*.	*easy easier easiest* *noisy noisier noisiest* *expensive **more** expensive **the most** expensive* *important **more** important **the most** important*
Repeat comparatives such as *more and more* and *better and better* to show that something is continuous.	*Members of this group are demonstrating **more and more** behavioral similarities across a range of countries and cultures.*
You use *the ... the* to show that one thing depends on another.	***The** older and wealthier Gen Y consumers become, **the** more important it is for companies to understand them.*
Don't forget some adjectives are irregular.	*good better best* ***bad worse worst***

1 **Complete this text with the comparative or superlative form of the adjectives in the box.**

busy	cheap	expensive	famous	formal	large	luxurious	quiet	small	young

In 1894, Charles Henry Harrod started what is perhaps today the (1) _____ department store in the world—everybody knows about it. The original store was much (2) _____ then than it is today—it only had one room. Now Harrods has developed into a much (3) _____ store offering food, stationery, cosmetics, and medicines. Today, Harrods sells some of the world's (4) _____ products, and if you're feeling rich, the (5) _____ product sold in Harrods is a £100 million yacht. Things can be much (6) _____ during the sales, but this is when Harrods is at its (7) _____, with people everywhere. So if you want a (8) _____ and more relaxing time, avoid the sales. However, remember to check the store rules before you go. If you are (9) _____ than 15, you have to go with an adult. Don't go to the store in your running shorts—you need to wear (10) _____ clothes than that.

2 **Correct the sentences below, paying attention to the use of *the ... the ...* and repeated comparatives such as *more and more*.**

1 Better your products are, the easier it will be to attract consumers.
2 Taller and tallest buildings are constructed every decade.
3 Consumers are getting more and more better at finding the cheapest prices online.
4 As Internet shopping becomes more important, the more flexible retailers will need to be.

WRITING TASK

Write a paragraph comparing two different types of consumer behavior.

BRAINSTORM

1 Read this paragraph. What is being compared? <u>Underline</u> the complex sentences.

¹Men and women shop in very different ways. ²One major difference is the factor of time. ³While men tend to make their buying decisions based on immediate needs, women are more likely to purchase something because it can be used again and again over time. ⁴Although men also consider the usefulness of the product for the long term future, this factor is less important for them. One similarity between the genders is that both men and women believe that expensive products tend to be better quality.

2 Think about the consumer behavior of two people from different generations in your family. Write notes on where they shop, what they buy, and how they shop.

PLAN

Plan your paragraph. Look back at what you wrote for the brainstorm section and write a sentence about the main idea of the paragraph. Decide how you want to organize your paragraph.

WRITE

Write a paragraph describing the similarities and differences between the two people and their consumer behavior. Pay attention to your use of comparatives, superlatives, and comparison/contrast language. Your paragraph should be 100–150 words long.

SHARE

Exchange paragraphs with a partner. Look at the checklist on page 109 and provide feedback to your partner.

REWRITE AND EDIT

Consider your partner's comments and rewrite your paragraph.

Common features of all academic writing

by Stella Cottrell

Although the wording of essay or other assignment titles may differ, almost all academic writing requires you to do certain things.

Use source materials

Do not simply state your personal opinion or say what is in your head. Instead, use material from reading, lecture notes, and other sources to give reasons, evidence, examples, and case studies.

Compare and contrast

Most assignments require some element of comparing and contrasting, especially of theories, models, or research findings. You will probably have to read different opinions and weigh them against each other.

Use criteria to evaluate

State which criteria you use to evaluate evidence: for example, that you are using the most up-to-date figures, or figures drawn from the largest survey, or a well-known expert's opinion for a particular reason (such as that he uses evidence from 20 well-conducted experiments).

Show awareness of complexities

Demonstrate that you are aware that answers are not always clear-cut. For example, although the expert you quote seems to have the best argument, his 20 experiments may all have used small children whereas the question set refers to teenagers. Acknowledge weaknesses in your own argument and strengths in opposing arguments. State clearly why there are difficulties coming to a firm conclusion one way or another.

Follow an argument

In your writing, show a line of reasoning which gives direction to the writing, so that one point follows logically from another.

Make a decision

Show which side of the argument, or which model or theory, is best in the final analysis. Even though the case may be fairly evenly weighted, show that you are able to make a decision on the basis of the evidence.

Follow a set structure

There is likely to be a set structure for the type of writing and a particular style for your subject area. *All* academic writing requires that you group similar points together in one paragraph or section, rather than scattering them through the text.

Be "discursive"

Link your points so that they feed into sentences and paragraphs, and so that each paragraph follows naturally from the previous one. All should contribute to a central guiding line of reasoning. (This is different from presenting a random set of points, for example, or headings with bullet points under them.)

Be emotionally neutral

Most academic writing requires you to stand back and analyze dispassionately, as an objective onlooker.

READING	Identifying main ideas
	Identifying cause and effect
VOCABULARY	Finding synonyms
WRITING	Combining facts and dates
GRAMMAR	The past progressive

Discussion point

Discuss these questions with a partner.

1 Look at these quotations about success. Which do you agree with? Why?

"Discouragement and failure are two of the surest stepping stones to success."

"Success is simply a matter of luck. Ask any failure."

"Winning isn't everything, it's the only thing."

I agree with ... because ...

2 Are successful people lucky? What role does luck play in success?

Luck is important because ...
I don't think luck plays a major role in success because ...

Vocabulary preview

Read the sentences. Match the words in bold with their meanings.

1 He never gives up in difficult situations, he always **perseveres**.
2 Losing my job was a major **setback** in my career.
3 Some people are born with a **talent**, but others simply work hard.
4 Successful people often recognize the **potential** of an idea before others.
5 Many inventors do not have the **opportunity** to make their ideas a reality because other technology is not advanced enough.
6 The **value** of an idea is not always seen until it becomes profitable.

a   to continue trying to achieve something difficult
b   a problem that delays or that stops progress or makes a situation worse
c   a chance to do something
d   the possibility to develop or achieve something in the future
e   the degree to which someone or something is important or useful
f   a natural ability for being good at a particular activity

1 Jean-Paul Gaultier   2 Bill Gates
3 Michael Jordan   4 Pierre Omidyar
5 Akio Morita   6 Mark Zuckerberg
7 Steven Spielberg   8 Oprah Winfrey

READING 1   What does it take to be successful?

Before you read

Work with a partner. Match the people with the product or thing they are associated with.

basketball   eBay™   Facebook   fashion   Microsoft®   movies
Sony®   television

Global reading

> ### IDENTIFYING MAIN IDEAS
>
> To identify the main ideas of a text, first look at the title, introduction, and any headings. These will give you clues about the topic and the main ideas. Then skim quickly over each section, paying particular attention to the first sentences. Make a note of the main ideas and look back at these notes after you have read the text again.

1 Read *What does it take to be successful?* and identify the four main sections.

2 Which sections of the text do you think these main ideas come from?
   1 Hard work and never giving up are key to success.
   2 To be successful, it is important to love what you do.
   3 Successful people can see what they want to achieve.
   4 Successful people use their imagination to see opportunities.

Close reading

Complete the statements about the article with no more than three words.

1 Having a vision is important because it gives you _____ your mind to work towards.
2 One benefit of experiencing setbacks is learning _____.
3 Successful people think of problems as _____.
4 In order to succeed, you must _____ what you do.

What does it take to be successful?

Home | About | Stories | Message board

1 Many books have been written about the secrets of success. But what special qualities do successful people have in common? Four key attributes stand out.

2 **Vision** Successful people visualize what they want. They have a picture in their mind of what their business will be like when they achieve their goals. This allows them to make decisions that support their vision.

3 Bill Gates' vision was to "put a computer on every desktop and in every home." At the time he was developing his first models, computers were very large, expensive, and mainly used in offices and factories. Most people couldn't see what Gates saw: that computers could have a value for personal uses. Today, most of us can't imagine life without a computer, and Microsoft has grown into a multi-billion-dollar company.

4 A talented programmer, Mark Zuckerberg had a vision for connecting people online. He was so convinced of his vision he even dropped out of college to develop it. In just a few years, Facebook became the most popular social networking site in the world.

5 **Persistence** Success doesn't come easily. Successful people are disciplined and persevere through failure. A key benefit of failure is to learn from your mistakes and persist through them. You won't find one successful person who hasn't experienced any setbacks.

6 Oprah Winfrey is one of the world's most successful women in television, but she was once fired from her job as a television reporter. Most people wouldn't believe that the best basketball player of all time was cut from his high school team. Michael Jordan says, "I have missed more than 9,000 shots in my career. I have lost almost 300 games. … I have failed over and over and over again in my life. And that is why I succeed."

7 **Creativity** Where other people see problems and limitations, successful people see possibilities and opportunities. When Akio Morita, the co-founder of Sony, developed a tape recorder, he had great difficulty in selling it because people could not see a use for it. After observing people in their daily lives, he realized people spent hours traveling and walking, and so he adapted his design to become the world famous Walkman®.

8 When the web took off in the mid-1990s, computer programmer Pierre Omidyar worried that big business would be a barrier to individual commerce. He saw the potential of the Internet to connect people around the world instantly. So Omidyar created eBay, a hugely successful online market where individuals compete with big companies.

9 **Passion** Successful people love what they do. Celebrity designer Jean-Paul Gaultier had no formal training in design, but loved creating clothing and at a young age began sending his drawings to famous French designers. One of these designers recognized his talent and hired him as an assistant. Later, he launched his own line of clothing and quickly became a global success.

10 Arguably all successful people have a mixture of vision, persistence, creativity, and passion, and one particular example is the director Steven Spielberg. From the age of eight he was making movies on a home video camera, and he won awards while he was still in school. However, his poor school grades made it difficult for him to get accepted to a top college, and eventually he dropped out of college altogether, sidetracked by his passion for film making. Every day he would sneak into a Universal Studios location trying to make contacts and get known, and he was frequently thrown out. Eventually, his talents led to him becoming one of the most successful directors in movie history.

11 Talented individuals do not necessarily make successful ones since talent alone is not enough. However, talent combined with passion, vision, persistence, and creativity is a potent force for success.

Developing critical thinking

Discuss these questions in a group.

1 Which quality do you think is the most important factor in success? Why?

The most important factor is … because …

2 Is just one of these qualities enough to be successful? Why or why not?

I think … is all you need to be successful because …

ACADEMIC KEYWORDS		
difficulty	(n)	/ˈdɪfɪkəlti/
limitation	(n)	/ˌlɪmɪˈteɪʃ(ə)n/
necessarily	(adv)	/ˌnesəˈserəli/

READING 2 Did they just get lucky?

Before you read

1 What's the luckiest thing that has happened to you? Do you think you were just fortunate, or were other factors like hard work and careful preparation more important?

2 Do you think that luck is an important factor in determining success?

I think most successful people are just lucky because ...

Global reading

1 Read *Did they just get lucky?* and match the people with the inventions.

1	William Perkin	___	a	penicillin
2	John Pemberton	___	b	Coca Cola®
3	Alexander Fleming	___	c	artificial colors for clothing

2 Who was actually trying to develop these products?

a cure for headaches   b malaria treatment

Close reading

▉ IDENTIFYING CAUSE AND EFFECT ▉

Texts about science often examine the reasons (or causes) why something happens and what happens as a result (or effects). These causes and effects are usually clearly indicated by signal words such as *because, because of, cause, due to, a reason, result in*. For example:

         cause   *effect*

His experiments **resulted in** a thick, cloudy liquid.

Sometimes the cause and effect are reversed:

         effect   *cause*

You can't make it at home **because** the recipe is still a secret.

1 Read these sentences adapted from the text. Match the causes with their effects.

Causes		Effects
1 The vibrant color didn't fade.	___	a He made a thick, cloudy liquid instead.
2 Fleming accidentally left some dishes open while he was away.	___	b It was better than natural dye.
3 Perkin was trying to come up with artificial quinine.	___	c Mold grew on some of them.

2 Look at these sentences. Match pairs of sentences, and decide which is a cause and which is an effect. Write *C* (cause) or *E* (effect).

a Bacteria didn't grow in those places.   ___

b The discovery made chemistry lucrative.   ___

c The signature red logo has barely changed since it was created.   ___

d It's one of the world's most recognized brands.   ___

e There was some mold in the dishes.   ___

f The field became attractive to many more people.   ___

Not all success comes down to perseverance. Louis Pasteur once said, "chance favors the prepared mind." Many popular inventions began as accidents. But the famous biologist and chemist knew there's a lot more to an "accident" than meets the eye. These successful inventors had the vision to see the potential in a failure, setback, or something that happens by chance.

Eighteen-year-old chemist William Perkin was looking for a cure for malaria. Instead, his experiments changed fashion forever.

In 1856, Perkin was trying to come up with artificial quinine, a drug that is used in malaria treatments. But his experiments resulted in a thick, cloudy liquid instead. Perkin didn't let his failed experiment stop him; rather, he saw a beautiful color in the mess and found that he could use it to change the color of clothes permanently. He had produced the first-ever synthetic dye. This dye was better than natural dye due to its bright color that didn't fade.

Suddenly businesses became interested in the work of scientists, and because his discovery made the field of chemistry profitable, it became attractive to a whole new generation. Not only did Perkin help to raise the profile of science, his "failure" has also helped fight cancer. While he was looking for a substance to assist with his groundbreaking work in chemotherapy in the 1870s, Paul Ehrlich, a German scientist, used Perkin's dyes.

In the late 1800s, pharmacist John Pemberton was trying to find a cure for headaches. He combined a variety of ingredients and came up with a thick, sweet liquid, which he mixed with carbonated water. It didn't cure headaches, but it tasted delicious. Pemberton saw an opportunity and started selling his drink in 1887 at a local drugstore soda fountain. It remained there for eight years before his business finally took off.

Today, the company sells more than 1.8 billion drinks every day worldwide. Its red logo has barely changed since it was created, which is one of the reasons it's one of the world's most recognized brands. But you can't make it at home because the recipe is still a secret, more than 125 years later! The mysterious drink? Coca Cola.

No story about chance discoveries is complete without the most famous and fortunate accident of the twentieth century. Biologist Alexander Fleming was heading off on vacation one day in 1928, and was too rushed to put away his work. When he came back, he realized he'd accidentally left open some dishes. But his mistake had caused something interesting to happen. There was a moldy growth on some of his dishes, and because of the mold, bacteria didn't grow in those places.

He saw the scientific implications and quickly tested his idea. The penicillin mold Fleming had discovered by chance became the first antibiotic and is still one of the most widely used antibiotics today.

Did they just GET LUCKY?

Developing critical thinking

1 Discuss the questions in a group.

1 Why do some people succeed and others fail?

The reason people succeed is …
The difference between success and failure is …

2 What role does failure play in success? How can mistakes and setbacks turn out to be successes? Give examples.

Failure can be positive because …
One example of a mistake turning out to be a success is …

ACADEMIC KEYWORDS

complete	(adj)	/kəmˈplit/
implication	(n)	/ˌɪmplɪˈkeɪʃ(ə)n/
widely	(adv)	/ˈwaɪdli/

2 Think about the ideas from *What does it take to be successful?* and *Did they just get lucky?* and discuss these questions in a group.

1 Do you think the inventors in *Did they just get lucky?* were just fortunate or did they show qualities such as passion, creativity, vision, and perseverance? If so, which was more important?

... was more important because ...

2 Think about your own experiences in life. What has most influenced your successes and why?

One success was ...
I think it was due to ... because ...

THINK ABOUT

friends   parents
hard work   practice
luck

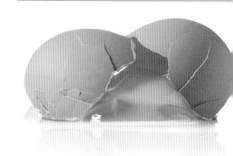

Vocabulary skill

▌ FINDING SYNONYMS

Synonyms are words or phrases that have similar meanings. Writers often use synonyms to avoid overusing words in a text. Often, an important word is explained, defined, or repeated as a synonym. If you don't know the meaning of a word, try to find its synonym in the text. If you can't find a synonym, try to guess its meaning from context. Sometimes, you will need to look up the word in a dictionary.

1 Find these sentences in *What does it take to be successful?* Then find synonyms in the text for the words in bold.

1 Four key **attributes** stand out. (paragraph 1) _____

2 Successful people **visualize** what they want. (paragraph 2) _____

3 Successful people are disciplined and **persevere** through failure. (paragraph 5) _____

4 You won't find one successful person who hasn't experienced any **setbacks**. (paragraph 5) _____

5 Where other people see problems and **limitations**, successful people see possibilities and opportunities. (paragraph 7–8) _____

2 Complete the sentences below with the words in bold from exercise 1.

1 She has the _____ to achieve top marks in the exam if she works harder.

2 Her greatest _____ is her creativity.

3 Sports people should always _____ their team winning before they play.

4 Technological _____ have stopped some people pursuing their ideas.

5 It can be challenging to overcome _____, but ultimately this may lead to success.

6 If he had _____ for a few more years, he may have been successful eventually.

WRITING Writing a personal statement

You are going to learn about describing people and events in the past, and using the past progressive. You are then going to use this language to write a paragraph in a personal statement.

Writing skill

■ COMBINING FACTS AND DATES ■

When you describe people and events in the past, combine facts and dates in different ways to add variety and interest to your sentences. For example, you can identify people in several ways.

Mark Zuckerberg was a talented programmer. He had a vision for connecting people online.

Mark Zuckerberg, a talented programmer, had a vision …
Talented programmer Mark Zuckerberg had a vision …
A talented programmer, Mark Zuckerberg, had a vision …

Dates can also go in various parts of a sentence.

Alexander Fleming was a biologist. One day in 1928, he was heading off on vacation. He was too rushed to put away his work.

One day in 1928, Alexander Fleming, a biologist, was heading off on vacation and …
Biologist Alexander Fleming was heading off on vacation one day in 1928, and …

1 **Look at the facts below. Use the words in italics to combine the facts into one sentence.**

1 The web took off in the mid-1990s.
   Pierre Omidyar, a computer programmer, worried that big business would be a barrier to individual commerce.

   When the web took off _____.

2 Paul Ehrlich was a German scientist.
   In the 1870s, he used Perkin's dyes to do groundbreaking work in chemotherapy.

   Paul Ehrlich, _____.

3 John Pemberton was a pharmacist.
   In the late 1800s, Pemberton was trying to find a cure for headaches.

   In the late 1800s, _____.

4 In 1887, Pemberton started selling his drink at a local drugstore soda fountain.
   The drink remained there for eight years before his business finally took off.

   Pemberton started selling his drink _____.

5 Fleming discovered the penicillin mold by chance.
   The penicillin mold became the first antibiotic.
   The antibiotic is still one of the most widely used antibiotics today.

   The penicillin mold Fleming had discovered _____.

Alexander Fleming

2 **Find the sentences in *What does it take to be successful?* and *Did they just get lucky?* that match 1–5 in exercise 1. Compare them with your sentences and note any differences.**

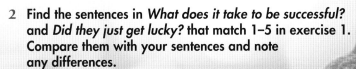

Grammar

THE PAST PROGRESSIVE

The past progressive tense is used to talk about events in progress in the past or to present background information in a narrative. It is also used to talk about longer actions that are happening around now and will continue in the future.

Form	Example
subject + *was/were* + VERB-*ing*	*Eighteen-year-old chemist William Perkin* **was looking** *for a cure for malaria.*

You use the past progressive for events that were in progress when another event occurred. You use the simple past to describe this event. You can use *while* to signal the event in progress. You can use *when* to signal the event that interrupted it.

While *John Pemberton* **was attempting** *to find a cure for headaches, he invented a delicious drink.*

John Pemberton **was attempting to find** *a cure for headaches* **when** *he invented a delicious drink.*

You use the past progressive when two events are in progress at the same time.

While *Mark Zuckerberg* **was developing** *his business, his classmates* **were still finishing** *their college degrees.*

1 Correct the mistakes in the sentences.

1 The students was waiting for the professor to begin the presentation.

2 Fareed was writing his assignment when the phone was ringing.

3 I'm sorry, I wasn't hearing what you said. I was reading this article for my essay.

4 I saw Cristina yesterday. She studied in the library.

5 The students discussed the results of the experiment when the bell rang.

2 Complete the summaries with the simple past or the past progressive form of the verbs.

1 In the late 1960s, a chemist named Spencer Silver _____ (try) to make a stronger, stickier glue when he _____ (create) the weak adhesive used in stick-on notes.

2 While an amateur Swiss inventor and his dog _____ (hike) in the mountains, he _____ (notice) that the seeds of a particular plant stuck to his dog and clothing. He _____ (invent) Velcro®, a hook-and-loop fastener that is very popular today.

3 A Japanese crime investigator _____ (work) on a murder case. While he _____ (look) at a slide under a microscope, he _____ (discover) that superglue "lifted" his fingerprint from the slide.

4 Charles Goodyear _____ (look) for ways to make rubber easier to work with, and improve its resistance to heat and cold. One day while he _____ (work), he _____ (spill) a mixture of rubber, sulfur, and lead onto a hot stove. Today, he is famous for developing the rubber used in tires.

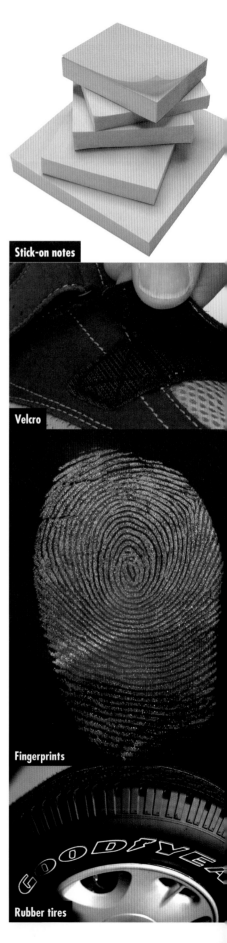

Stick-on notes

Velcro

Fingerprints

Rubber tires

WRITING TASK

Write about a challenge or setback you have experienced, and how you overcame them to show your ability to succeed.

BRAINSTORM

1 Read the paragraph. Circle the verbs in the simple past and underline the verbs in the past progressive.

My determination to succeed has been met with many challenges. My first challenge came when I decided to go to college. None of my friends decided to go to college, and while I was applying and preparing to go, we grew apart. During the first year of my master's program, I changed jobs, and my wife and I had twins. While I was writing my master's thesis, I also had to deal with a lot of pressure in my new job. While I was working hard to meet all my targets in my job, and help my wife take care of our children, I completed my master's program with top grades. Last year, I completed my Ph.D. When I was walking across the stage to receive my diploma, I realized with great pride that accomplishing any dream takes a lot of perseverance and determination.

2 What obstacles have you met or setbacks have you experienced in your life? How did you overcome them? Brainstorm a list and write your ideas in the chart.

Obstacles, setbacks, challenges	Ways you overcame them

PLAN

Plan a paragraph that shows how you can overcome obstacles. Look at the chart above and choose the best example.

1 Write one sentence that states that you have persevered through one or more challenges.
2 Write a sentence that describes the challenge you experienced.
3 Now make a list of the steps you took to overcome the challenge.

WRITE

Write your paragraph. Be honest but positive. What did you learn from going through this? Your paragraph should be 100–150 words long.

SHARE

Exchange paragraphs with a partner. Look at the checklist on page 109 and provide feedback to your partner.

REWRITE AND EDIT

Consider your partner's comments and rewrite your paragraph.

STUDY SKILLS Editing your own work

Getting started

Discuss these questions with a partner.

1 Do you check your work after you have written it? What things do you look for?
2 Do you ask someone else to read your work? Who and why?
3 How many drafts or versions do you usually write? Why are drafts an important part of the writing process?

Scenario

Read this scenario and think about what Akiko did right and what she did wrong.

Consider it

Read the tips about editing your work. Discuss each one with a partner. Why do you think each one is important?

1 **Line of argument** Read your essay and check your main argument is clear in your introduction. Every paragraph should then refer back to your main argument. Try adding one sentence to show how each paragraph connects.
2 **Paragraphs** Read each paragraph and check it has one main point. Everything in the paragraph should be related to and support this main point. If there is more than one point in a paragraph, you will need to put the additional points into new paragraphs, making sure the connection to your main argument is clear.
3 **References** Check that you have referenced all your sources and listed them correctly in the bibliography.
4 **Academic style** Check your work is written in a formal and neutral style. Pay attention to differences between academic English and spoken/ informal English. Exclamation marks, contracted forms (e.g., *there's*), and informal vocabulary (e.g., *lots of* instead of *many*) are some examples of informal style to look out for. It is often more appropriate to use passives in formal writing.
5 **Language** Check your work carefully for grammar, punctuation, and spelling mistakes. Do not rely just on a spell checker—*two* and *tow* are both spelt correctly, but they have completely different meanings.

Over to you

Discuss these questions with a partner.

1 What do you think is more important—accurate language or coherent structure?
2 How many drafts do you do of an essay?
3 Do you look at different things each time or do you try to deal with everything at once?

Akiko finished the first draft of her essay a week before the deadline. She was quite happy with it, and had spent a long time researching and writing it. Once she had finished the first draft, she checked her grammar and spelling thoroughly, and corrected the mistakes. She considered the style and decided that some of it was too informal, so she changed some of the words and phrases she'd used. Akiko was really pleased because she thought her English was excellent in the essay. The night before the deadline, she asked her friend to check it. To her surprise, her friend couldn't understand the essay. Akiko's friend told her the meaning wasn't clear and that the ideas were organized in a confusing way. When she read her essay more carefully she noticed that each paragraph had multiple topics. Her main argument wasn't clear and it wasn't obvious how her paragraphs linked back to it. She had only focused on her language at the draft stage and had forgotten to check for other key issues. She didn't have time to make changes now. Akiko got a low mark in the essay. The comment from the teacher said "Lacks coherence."

Pressure

READING	Taking notes: Using your own words
	Identifying tone
	Researching an essay
VOCABULARY	Opinion adverbs
WRITING	Expanding notes into summaries
GRAMMAR	Present conditionals

Discussion point

Discuss these questions with a partner.

1 Look at the picture. Why do you think the man looks so stressed?

He is probably stressed because ...

2 What other things make people stressed? Why?

Many people find ... stressful.
These things make people stressed because ...

3 What makes you stressed? Think about the words in the box.

| family | money | technology | work/study |

I get most stressed about ...

Vocabulary preview

Ⓒircle the correct words to complete the text about what makes people feel stressed.

(1) **Pressure / Stress** is the worried feeling that you get when you have to deal with a difficult or complicated situation. One common area that puts people under (2) **pressure / impact** is work. With parents spending more time in the office, many families feel the (3) **strain / ambition** of a poor work-life balance. In many working environments, employees have to meet increasingly challenging targets to (4) **achieve / satisfy** their employers. Due to this, the (5) **impact / result** on an individual's physical and mental health can be significant. Many people feel a need to earn more money to ensure they can buy all the material goods they (6) **obtain / desire**—such as cars, clothes, and houses. This (7) **intention / ambition** places a constant pressure on people, because once they (8) **achieve / satisfy** one goal, it is quickly replaced by another material goal, and the cycle repeats itself.

READING 1 The stresses and strains of work

Before you read

Look at the list of jobs. Place them in order from 1–5, with 1 being the most stressful. Discuss the reasons for your choice with a partner.

I think … has a more/less stressful job than … because …

JOBS	
nurse	taxidermist
police officer	teacher
politician	

Global reading

Skim *The stresses and strains of work*. Choose the best summary.

1 Work can lead to a lot of stress in people's lives, especially for people who work in the IT sector. One study found that 80% of people in IT are stressed, and 25% have taken time off for stress. It is largely other people's lack of IT skills that make working in IT especially stressful.

2 Work can be one of the biggest causes of stress in people's lives. Jobs that are particularly stressful are in the areas of IT, medicine, engineering, sales and marketing, and education. Common factors that lead to stress are deadlines, job satisfaction, and doing other people's work. Many people want to quit their job to become self-employed, but this is also stressful.

3 Lots of jobs are very stressful, and it is mainly deadlines that make people stressed. Lots of people think self-employment is the best solution, but it probably isn't.

Close reading

TAKING NOTES: USING YOUR OWN WORDS

Taking notes in your own words is important. It will help you avoid potential plagiarism. If you take notes from a text using the same words, then repeat them in an essay, you could be plagiarizing by accident. Also, writing notes in your own words helps you understand what you are writing about, rather than just copying what you read.

3,000 people questioned by SWNS for SkillSoft.

97% people in IT stressed permanently

80% stressed prior to work

25% sick because of stress

1 Look at the notes on paragraph 2 of *The stresses and strains of work*. Read the paragraph again and <u>underline</u> the parts that are in the notes.

2 Read the text more carefully and take notes on the following topics.

  1 The most stressful thing about IT   **3** Disadvantages of self-employment

  2 The pressures of targets and deadlines   **4** Typical factors causing stress

THE STRESSES & STRAINS OF WORK

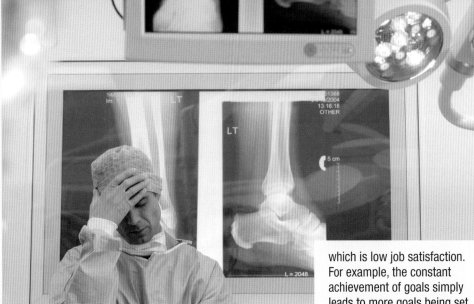

1 Because work takes up such a large proportion of people's lives, it is perhaps not surprising that it causes stress. At one time or another, most employees have felt the strain of work and have felt their job is just too stressful. However, what jobs in the world are the most stressful and what makes people in these jobs feel under so much pressure?

2 According to a poll of over 3,000 people, conducted by SWNS for SkillSoft, 97% of IT professionals feel the impact of stress every day. Eighty percent feel stressed before getting to work, and 25% have taken time off work because of stress. So what makes IT such a stressful profession?

3 The strain apparently comes from a variety of factors, one of which is other employees' poor IT skills. If you had to explain the most simple of procedures, such as how to access databases or download files several times every day, you might feel frustrated, too. Not only do IT professionals work with people who have little knowledge, but they also face pressure to achieve targets from managers.

4 Together with IT in the top five, the other most stressful professions are medicine, engineering, sales and marketing, and education. So what makes such a diverse range of jobs so challenging? Common areas of stress in all these professions are meeting deadlines, doing other people's work, and a feeling of low job satisfaction.

5 People working in all of these jobs have a range of targets to achieve and deadlines to meet in order to satisfy their employers. If you work in sales and marketing, you will almost certainly have to meet sales targets. If you are a teacher, you will have to meet deadlines for handing in students' grades. Or, if you are an engineer, you will have to meet project deadlines. A shortage of time seems to cause pressure in a wide range of professions.

6 Many of these professions are also highly skilled, and the work cannot be done by just anybody. Consequently, when a colleague is off sick or on vacation, the workload needs to be shared among a limited number of individuals, which places greater pressure on each individual's time. This perhaps contributes to the other common area, which is low job satisfaction. For example, the constant achievement of goals simply leads to more goals being set, and thus the cycle continues.

7 Apparently, a third of people want to quit their jobs to become self-employed. Many feel that if they were self-employed, they would have control over their working day and time. However, the grass isn't always greener on the other side. According to other surveys, self-employment is one of the most stressful methods of working—no matter what the job is. You aren't guaranteed a steady income, and if you aren't good at your job, you might find you don't have one. In the end, it may be worth dealing with the stress of work, rather than trying to find a different kind of job.

ACADEMIC KEYWORDS

knowledge (n)	/ˈnɑlɪdʒ/
proportion (n)	/prəˈpɔrʃ(ə)n/
surprising (adj)	/sərˈpraɪzɪŋ/

USEFUL LANGUAGE
colleagues
environment
job security
working hours

Developing critical thinking

Discuss these questions in a group.

1 What are the advantages and disadvantages of being self-employed compared to working for a company? Which would you prefer?

Being self-employed means ...

I would prefer ...

2 The survey in the text questioned 3,000 people, but what do we know about who these 3,000 people are? If we knew the following, how might it change our opinion?

a They are all employed by the same company.
b They all work in the same country.
c The company that commissioned the survey (SkillSoft) is an IT training company.

If I knew that ... this would make me think that maybe ...

READING 2 Rich and famous

Before you read

Discuss these questions with a partner.

1 What jobs do most young children in your country want to have?
   Do you think the following can be considered jobs?

   actor   athlete   pop star

   Being a ... is/isn't a job because ...

2 What problems might be caused if most children want to have jobs
   like these?

Global reading

> **IDENTIFYING TONE**
>
> The tone of a text can help you to identify and understand the writer's
> opinion. This is important if you plan to use the reading in an essay because
> it will give you an idea whether the writer is for or against a certain
> position. The author's opinion is often indicated by certain fixed phrases,
> and the author's choice of adjectives and adverbs.

1 **Read *Rich and famous* quickly and decide whether the author has a
   positive or negative opinion about the following topics.**

   1 the change in children's aspirations
   2 the wealth associated with sports stars, pop stars, and actors
   3 the belief that a celebrity lifestyle is easily attainable
   4 people's job aspirations in the past

2 **Read *Rich and famous* again and <u>underline</u> words and phrases that
   helped you identify the author's opinion.**

Close reading

> **TAKING NOTES: RESEARCHING AN ESSAY**
>
> In an academic situation, you will do a lot of your reading with a specific
> essay question in mind. When you are taking notes for a specific essay, it
> is a good idea to plan your research questions. This will help you to think
> about the questions you need to answer and make your reading and note
> taking more focused.

1 **Imagine you have to write an essay on the topic below. Discuss with
   a partner how *Rich and famous* might be useful in writing the essay.**

   People who aspire to fame and fortune often feel more pressure than happiness. Discuss.

2 **Work with a partner and note down three or four questions that would
   help you write the essay.**

   1 *How does trying to make money cause pressure?*
   2 _____
   3 _____
   4 _____

3 Read *Rich and famous* again and make notes answering your research questions from exercise 2.

If you could have any job in the world, what would it be? This is a common question throughout childhood in any culture. Children have been asked this question for generations, but it seems their answers are changing. A recent study has highlighted a dramatic and rather worrying shift in children's ambitions.

Twenty-five years ago, the most common aspiration of American children was to be a teacher, followed by working in banking and finance, and then medicine. Today's younger generation most commonly say they want to be a sports star, a pop star, or an actor. While many would argue that there is nothing wrong with having such ambitions, others feel that this trend will ultimately lead to dissatisfaction as more and more people are unable to reach their goals.

According to the survey, children desire these jobs largely because of the excessive wealth associated with them. However, according to experts, such ambitions are likely to place a strain on the individual. Julian Rotter, an American psychologist, proposed an aspiration theory, in which people assess how likely they are to achieve a goal before they make the effort to achieve it. If people link happiness to wealth and status, they are more likely to work hard to achieve them. However, the satisfaction is short-lived because once the goal has been met, the person no longer has a sense of satisfaction. This then creates a pressure for the person to keep pushing to achieve more targets, which places the individual under greater stress.

Unfortunately, fame and fortune do not always have a positive impact on an individual's life. Many careers in the spotlight are short-lived. For example, many athletes' physical peak only lasts a few years, and singers can have a very limited career. The field that was once the sole focus of their lives becomes something they have little or no involvement in. As a result, they have a feeling of worthlessness and a complete lack of control. It can also be difficult for them to adapt back to a normal everyday life because they have been so far removed from it for so long.

So despite the drawbacks of being rich and famous, there is greater ambition than ever among young people to attain that status. In many ways, this has been brought about by cultural changes. Globally, more and more TV shows feature talent competitions where winners can achieve wealth and fame in just a few weeks or months. This quick route to fame and fortune creates a celebrity culture. People unrealistically believe that a celebrity lifestyle is easily attainable and leads to great satisfaction. It is perhaps not surprising that this is especially attractive in societies where youth unemployment rates are between 25% and 50%.

It is no longer enough to have simple aspirations. People are not satisfied just making a living—they want to be rich. In the past, people had more modest, sensible aims such as earning a steady income, not being unemployed, and enjoying their work. Job satisfaction was important. Parents and teachers, rather than TV, had a greater impact on children's ambitions. Unfortunately not everyone realizes that it takes talent, skill, and hard work to be good at a sport or at singing. As a result, many people won't fulfill their childhood dreams, and this could have a negative effect on their happiness.

Rich and famous

Developing critical thinking

1 **Discuss these questions in a group.**

1 Do you think it is good for children to want to have the jobs described in the article? Why or why not?

2 According to Rotter, goals create pressure because once you achieve them they are replaced with new goals. Do you agree? Why or why not?

I agree that goals create stress because ...

2 **Think about the ideas from *The stresses and strains of work* and *Rich and famous* and discuss these questions in a group.**

1 Which do you think creates more pressure—trying to get the job you want or working at a job?

More pressure comes from ...

2 What stresses and pressures might be associated with being an athlete? Do you think these jobs would be more or less stressful than an IT career? Why?

Athletes have to deal with ...

ACADEMIC KEYWORDS		
despite	(prep)	/dɪˈspaɪt/
highlight	(v)	/ˈhaɪˌlaɪt/
ultimately	(adv)	/ˈʌltɪmətli/

USEFUL LANGUAGE	
attention	paparazzi
family	pressure to succeed
friends	privacy
money	trust

Vocabulary skill

OPINION ADVERBS

One common way an author can show an opinion on a topic is through using certain adverbs. Adverbs are often used to show certainty and doubt, to indicate a viewpoint, and to give an evaluation or assessment of a topic.

Unfortunately, fame and fortune do not always have a positive impact on an individual's life.

Because work takes up such a large proportion of people's lives, it is perhaps not surprising that it causes stress.

1 Match the adverbs with their meanings.

1	likely	____	a normally
2	undoubtedly	____	b probably going to happen, or probably true
3	typically	____	c used for saying that you wish that something will happen
4	apparently	____	d mainly
5	hopefully	____	e used for saying that something is certainly true or is accepted by everyone
6	unfortunately	____	f used for saying that something is sad or disappointing
7	largely	____	g based only on what you have heard, not on what you are certain is true
8	perhaps	____	h used for saying that you are not certain about something, or that something may or may not be true

2 Rewrite each sentence using an adverb from the box. The adverb should have the same meaning as the word(s) in parentheses.

> apparently   hopefully   largely   ~~likely~~   perhaps
> typically   undoubtedly   unfortunately

1 People are happier in less pressured jobs. (probably)
   People are likely to be happier in less pressured jobs.

2 Most people won't be rich and famous. (disappointingly)
   _____

3 IT professionals have to deal with people who do not understand computers. (usually)
   _____

4 People want more money nowadays. (definitely)
   _____

5 Movie stars are the wealthiest entertainers. (possibly)
   _____

6 Constant goal setting leads to more disappointment and pressure. (it has been said or written)
   _____

7 In the future, employers will implement measures to make their employees' lives less stressful. (we wish)
   _____

8 Children's career aspirations are based on becoming rich rather than finding job satisfaction. (mostly)
   _____

WRITING Writing a summary

You are going to learn about summary writing and using conditional sentences. You are then going to use these to write a paragraph summarizing *Rich and famous*.

Writing skill

EXPANDING NOTES INTO SUMMARIES

A good summary should be shorter than the original text but should not change the main meaning. It should also largely be written in your own words. Using your own words is especially important if you plan to use the summary in an essay; otherwise, you may plagiarize the text. A good summary should focus mostly on the main idea but will often also include any key supporting details. To ensure your summary is in your own words it is often best to take notes on a text and expand these notes into a summary.

1 **Look at these common words from the two texts and work with a partner to try to think of different ways of saying the same things.**

people — *individuals*   job — _____

achieve — _____   range — _____

satisfaction — _____   wealth — _____

stressful — _____   pressure — _____

2 **Look at the paragraph below and the notes taken on it. Underline the parts the writer has noted down.**

People working in all of these jobs have a range of targets to achieve and deadlines to meet in order to satisfy their employers. If you work in sales and marketing, you will almost certainly have to meet sales targets. If you are a teacher, you will have to meet deadlines for handing in students' grades. Or, if you are an engineer, you will have to meet project deadlines. A shortage of time seems to cause pressure in a wide range of professions.

meet goals and deadlines = happy boss. Stressful jobs = deadlines + limited time

3 **Look at how the notes have been expanded into a summary. Answer the questions that follow.**

Meeting goals and deadlines is the key to keeping your boss happy. All of these stressful jobs have a lot of deadlines and limited time to meet them.

1 How different is this from the original?
2 Is this student likely to be accused of plagiarizing?

4 **Use your notes from the *Close reading* section on page 58 to write a brief summary of *The stresses and strains of work*.**

5 **Compare your summaries with a partner. As you read your partner's summary, answer the questions below.**

1 Is it shorter than the original?
2 Is it written in your partner's own words?
3 Has it kept the same meaning?

Grammar

PRESENT CONDITIONALS

We use a different conditional depending on whether we are talking about a real or imaginary situation. We use the present real conditional to talk about events that are *likely* to happen, and the present unreal conditional to talk about events that are *unlikely* to happen.

Form	Example
Present real conditional *If* clause result clause present simple + *will* / another modal verb	*If you **remain** calm, you **may** just find out how powerful you really are.*
Present unreal conditional *If* clause result clause past simple + *would/might/could*	*If she **was** a doctor, she **would** be a lot more stressed.*

Conditional sentences can be a good way of providing a supporting example or explanation.

If you had to explain the simplest procedures, such as how to access databases or download files several times every day, you might feel frustrated, too.

1 **Complete the conditional sentences with the correct form of the verbs in parentheses.**

  1 If I _____ (work) hard, I _____ (get) promoted.
  2 If I _____ (graduate) with a good degree, I _____ (have) a better chance of a good job.
  3 I _____ (be) less stressed if I _____ (change) my job.
  4 If someone _____ (be) self-employed, they _____ (be) more stressed.
  5 If I _____ (not work), I _____ (feel) under even more pressure than I do now.

2 **Complete these present unreal conditional sentences so that they are true for you.**

  1 If I could have any job in the world, I …
  2 If I had my own business, it …
  3 I would feel less stressed if …
  4 If I could buy anything in the world, I …
  5 I would be happier if …
  6 If I was under pressure, I …

3 **Work with a partner and ask them questions to find out what they would do in each of the situations in exercise 2.**

WRITING TASK

Write a paragraph summarizing the main ideas from *Rich and famous*.

BRAINSTORM

1   Read the paragraph below that summarizes *The stresses and strains of work*. Identify where each part comes from in the main text and notice how the ideas are expressed differently. Make a note of any synonyms used. Which sentence uses a conditional? Is it a real or unreal conditional?

A survey by SWNS for SkillSoft has identified the IT sector as the most stressful to work in. Apparently, the stress comes from having to deal with other people's lack of IT skills on a daily basis, but also from doing the job under time pressure. All of the top five most stressful professions have these common features. If you have to meet deadlines, you will feel stressed. This is especially true when you have limited time. Many people hope to solve their stress issues by becoming self-employed. However, self-employment carries its own stresses and strains.

2   You are going to write a paragraph summarizing *Rich and famous*. Underline the most important points in the text. Now make notes in your own words.

PLAN

Look at your notes and check you have covered all the main points of the text. Decide how you want to organize your paragraph.

WRITE

Write a paragraph summarizing *Rich and famous*. Try to include one example using a conditional clause. Your paragraph should be 100–150 words long.

SHARE

Exchange paragraphs with a partner. Look at the checklist on page 109 and provide feedback to your partner.

REWRITE AND EDIT

Consider your partner's comments and rewrite your paragraph.

STUDY SKILLS Referencing and plagiarism

Getting started

Discuss these questions with a partner.

1 What information sources do we use when writing essays and assignments?
2 What information do you need to record in a text next to someone else's ideas?

Scenario

Read this scenario and decide what Lok did right and what she did wrong.

Consider it

Read the tips about research and referencing. Discuss each one with a partner. Do you do this already? Why is it important to do these things?

1 **Check the authority of the source** It's important when you use a source that you check its authority. This means you should check that the author is an expert in their field. On the internet, anyone can write anything even if they have little knowledge or expertise.

2 **Direct references** When you directly reference a source, use the exact words from a text. Put the information in quotation marks (" ") and/or indent the text. Also include the year of publication, page number, and author surname, e.g., (Brown, 2012:29)

3 **Indirect references** Indirect references use other people's own ideas but your words. You do not include quotation marks or the page number, but you should write the author's surname and year of publication.

4 **Direct or indirect?** In general, it is better to include more indirect than direct quotations. It shows better understanding of the text, and it will flow better with your own writing.

5 **Bibliography** At the end of an essay, it is important to include a full list of all sources you have used. This list contains more information than references in the text, for example:

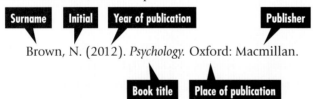

Brown, N. (2012). *Psychology.* Oxford: Macmillan.

When referencing a website, we also include the date accessed and the URL of the specific page, for example:

Gilbert, N. (2012). *Water Under Pressure.* Retrieved from: http://www.nature.com/news/water-under-pressure-1.10216 Accessed: 18/03/2012

6 **Check referencing conventions at your institution** Some institutions and departments prefer students to reference their sources in a particular way which may be different to the ways recommended here. Check with your teacher if you are unsure.

Over to you

Discuss these questions with a partner.

1 Do you think plagiarism is usually deliberate cheating?
2 Which of the points in the *Consider it* section are essential for avoiding accusations of plagiarism?

Lok knew that her teacher wanted her tutorial group to include six references in their essays. She spent a lot of time searching online and in the library. Lok found some good examples that helped her define key terms and support her arguments. They were academic sources written by experts and not from unreliable sources like blogs. She was worried that her English wasn't good enough, so she cut and pasted some paragraphs from the sources into her essay. She was sure this was fine, as it would just make her essay better, and she would get a high mark. Lok didn't have much time left to finish her essay, so she forgot to list the sources she had used at the end. When she got her essay back, she had failed the piece of work. She was given zero for plagiarism. Lok didn't understand why; she didn't think she had cheated and thought she had done what the teacher asked her to do.

READING	Using topic sentences
	Identifying supporting details
VOCABULARY	Verb and preposition collocations
WRITING	Developing paragraphs
GRAMMAR	The present perfect simple

Discussion point

Discuss these questions with a partner.

1 Look at the picture. How does it make you feel?

It makes me feel ...

2 What are you afraid of? Why?

I'm afraid of ... because ...

3 What do you think causes peoples' fears?

Some fears are caused by ...

Vocabulary preview

Match the words in bold with their definitions.

1 Doctors want to **cure** sick patients so that they are well again.
2 I find it hard to **cope** when I have too much to do.
3 I am trying to **confront** my fear of spiders by looking at pictures of them.
4 I **react** so badly to heights that they make me feel sick.
5 When did you **develop** your fear of flying?
6 Many fears are **innate** and come from the natural development of humans.
7 I **panic** if I see a large dog.
8 When I see a snake, I feel more than just fear; it's a real **phobia**.

a to begin to have something such as a problem or sickness
b a very strong feeling of disliking or being afraid of someone or something
c to stop someone being affected by an sickness; to control or get rid of a bad habit, feeling, or attitude
d to deal successfully with a difficult situation or job
e a quality or ability that you have always had
f to have a sudden strong feeling of fear or worry that makes you unable to think clearly or calmly
g to behave in a particular way because of something that is happening around you or something that someone is doing
h to face up to and deal with a difficult situation

READING 1 Fears, reactions, coping

Before you read

Look at these common fears. Try to rank them in order from the most common to the least common fear. Discuss your ideas with a partner.

The most common fear is probably ...

COMMON FEARS	
heights	storms
public transportation	water
snakes	

Global reading

USING TOPIC SENTENCES

The topic sentence is usually the first sentence of a paragraph, but it might be the second or third sentence. It introduces the main idea of the paragraph and all other ideas in the paragraph will be related to the topic sentence. You can use topic sentences to help you locate the information you need more quickly.

1 **Read the topic sentences below. Look through *Fears, reactions, coping* quickly and try to match the topic sentences with the paragraphs in the text.**

1 There are many fears that have developed from our natural human responses to dangerous situations.
2 So how many people suffer from phobias?
3 We all like to think that we are different, but our fears are very similar.
4 Fortunately, there are many ways to cope with fears and phobias.
5 However, many of our fears are not innate; they are learned from our experiences.

2 <u>Underline</u> **the words or ideas that helped you match the sentences with each paragraph.**

Close reading

1 **Look at paragraph 3 in *Fears, reactions, coping* and identify the function of each sentence.**

1 However, many of …
2 For example, if …
3 Or, if a parent …
4 The reason …

2 **Find examples in *Fears, reactions, coping* of the following things.**

1 common fears
2 situations that caused humans to develop innate fears
3 fears that are learned from experience
4 two specific phobias
5 one social phobia

FEARS, REACTIONS, COPING

1

Many people have a fear of things like snakes, spiders, heights, water, and small enclosed spaces. If many people have the same fears, how do we all develop them?

2

If you think about the time when we did not live in houses, but alongside nature, we faced many more dangers from animals. We have developed a response to situations that might cause us harm, such as a bite from a poisonous snake or a bite from a dog. Of course, not all fears are innate.

3

For example, if you see someone almost drown, you may react by developing a fear of water. Or, if a parent has a fear of heights, it is quite common for their children to also develop a fear of heights. The reason for this is not genetic; it is simply because children learn behavior and attitudes from their parents.

4

To answer this question, we have to define what is meant by *phobia*. While almost everyone has a fear of something, whether it is spiders or flying, a fear is only classified as a phobia by psychologists if it is so serious it affects your daily life. According to the Anxiety Disorders Association of America, 19 million Americans (around 6% of the population) have specific phobias, such as crossing bridges or going through tunnels. Another 15 million (around 5%) have a social phobia such as public speaking. Unfortunately, those who have one phobia are likely to have others, too.

5

Because many fears are learned during our lives, we simply have to unlearn these feelings. If people confront their fear in a gradual way, they can learn to control how they react to the situation and not panic. It might not cure the fear completely, but it will probably help people to cope better.

Developing critical thinking

Discuss these questions in a group.

1 Do you think fears are something to worry about, or are they just a natural part of life? Why or why not?

   As far as I'm concerned, people shouldn't worry about phobias because …
   I definitely feel that if a fear is very strong, it's a problem because …

2 Discuss with a partner which of the following suggestions is the best solution to a fear of public speaking. Why?

   a Take deep breaths with your eyes closed.
   b Focus on other people.
   c Imagine yourself in a place where you are happy.
   d Don't worry about being perfect.

   The best solution is probably … because …

ACADEMIC KEYWORDS		
simply	(adv)	/ˈsɪmpli/
social	(adj)	/ˈsoʊʃ(ə)l/
whether	(conj)	/ˈweðər/

READING 2 Superhuman powers

Before you read

Discuss these questions with a partner.

1 When was the last time you were scared? How did you react?

The last time I was scared was when ...
I felt ...

2 Do you ever react in a positive way to fear?

I react positively when ...

Global reading

1 **Look at *Superhuman powers*. Is it:**

a a news story about fans of comic book heroes?

b a magazine article about the "powers" we all possess?

2 **Read the topic sentences of each paragraph in *Superhuman powers* and identify in which paragraph you could find the information to answer these questions.**

1 Why do we react quickly to danger?

2 Why does time pass slowly when we are faced with danger?

3 Is fear always negative?

4 Why doesn't danger worry some people?

5 How do we react physically to fear?

6 What makes us focus on the situation so much?

3 **Read *Superhuman powers* again and answer the questions in exercise 2.**

Close reading

> ### ■ IDENTIFYING SUPPORTING DETAILS
>
> Supporting details are used to give the reader a clearer understanding of the topic. When a topic sentence is not clear, identifying the supporting sentences may help you to understand a paragraph more fully.

Read *Superhuman powers* again and answer the questions, using supporting details in the paragraphs.

1 What can't we do well under pressure?

2 How much strength do we normally use, and when do we use more?

3 What example does the text give of a situation where we focus our mind more?

4 Why does it seem as if time is slower when we are in a dangerous situation?

5 How do we feel when a dangerous situation is over?

6 What might we find out when faced with a dangerous situation?

7 Which reaction does the author think we know the least about?

ACADEMIC KEYWORDS

extreme	(adj)	/ɪkˈstriːm/
immediate	(adj)	/ɪˈmiːdiət/
tend	(v)	/tend/

1 **Most people** associate fear with negative feelings, but it can actually be very positive as well. Fear is something innate that we actually rely on to keep us safe when faced with danger. If we are confronted with a dangerous situation, we can unlock abilities that we often do not know we have. Understanding these secret superpowers can help you react to difficult situations in a better way.

2 **In the** past, humans faced danger on a daily basis so they learned to respond to it instantly in order to stay alive. Today the brain still reacts in the same way and makes you respond to a situation so quickly that you do it before you are aware of the situation. How you respond depends on the situation. If the danger is immediate, a person might run or fight. If it's far away, the reaction might be to freeze (stand still).

3 **Our response** not only becomes faster when we are faced with danger, but we also benefit from fear by becoming stronger in dangerous situations. Under pressure, skills such as putting a key in a door usually become worse, but physical skills such as running and jumping tend to improve. If an angry dog chases you, you will probably run faster. In a normal situation, we often only use 65% of our strength, but studies have shown that this can increase to as much as 85% in more dangerous situations.

4 **When an** immediate threat appears, our mind focuses on the things that are really important. The brain releases chemicals that make the mind more alert and active when attention is needed. If you know you are about to speak in front of 200 people, you are likely to be thinking about nothing else other than what you want to say. You are unlikely to be thinking about what you are going to have for dinner tonight.

5 **When people** have faced a fear, some have commented on the feeling of time slowing down—something that actually lasts for one or two seconds can feel like 20 or 30 seconds. Obviously, time does not actually slow down, so what is happening to our brain? Well, no one knows for sure, but some attribute the feeling of time slowing down to the part of the brain that creates a more detailed memory. So when we look back at the event, the details make it feel like it lasted a long time.

6 **The final** superpower is one of fearlessness, in other words, not being worried or concerned about the situation. When faced with the most extreme dangers, many people do not actually feel scared at all. There is often a feeling of complete calm and almost no emotional reaction. It is only later, once the threat has gone, that people start to panic and feel nervous.

7 **So if you** find yourself in extreme danger in the future, remember the superhuman strengths we all possess. Whether it is strength, speed, or fearlessness that helps you, if you remain calm, you might just find out how powerful you really are.

SUPERHUMAN
POWERS

Developing critical thinking

1 **Discuss these questions in a group.**

1 How might fear be positive in each of the situations in the box on the right?

Fear could be positive when … because …
I think fear would help you if you were … because …

2 Do you agree that fear can be positive? Why?

I think fear can be positive because …
In my opinion, fear is always negative because …

THINK ABOUT
Being near a dangerous snake
Giving a presentation
Running a race
Taking an exam

2 **Think about the ideas from *Fears, reactions, coping* and *Superhuman powers* and discuss these questions in a group.**

1 Do you think we learn fears and reactions to them, or are we born with them?

It could be argued that … because …

2 Of the most common fears described in *Fears, reactions, coping*, how might the reactions in *Superhuman powers* help someone deal with the situation positively?

For people who are scared of … they could help by …

Vocabulary skill

VERB AND PREPOSITION COLLOCATIONS

Many words commonly collocate with (are used together with) another word. Collocations are sometimes the same in different languages, but sometimes they are different. For example, in some languages you *do a mistake,* but in others, like English, you *make a mistake.* For accuracy, it is important to learn which words go together. Learning collocations also helps you build your vocabulary more quickly.

A number of verbs commonly collocate with prepositions. This means a particular preposition typically comes after a particular verb. For example:

*Many people actually **benefit from** feelings of fear.*

In some cases, an object of the verb can come between the verb and the preposition. For example:

*We **associate** it **with** feelings of panic and stress.*

1 **Look at the following verb and preposition collocations from *Superhuman powers* and try to guess their meaning from the context.**

When people **comment on** fear, they often **focus on** the negatives, and **associate** fear **with** feelings of panic and stress. However, our survival can **depend on** how we **react to** a dangerous situation. Many people actually **benefit from** feelings of fear and sometimes even **attribute** their success **to** it.

2 **Replace the phrase in *italics* with a collocation from exercise 1. You may need to change the grammatical form.**

1 The way she *responds to* feedback is very negative.
2 He *relies on* other people a lot for help.
3 People with phobias *can see an improvement by* visiting a doctor.
4 Fear is often *linked to* something we have learned from our experiences in life.
5 She always *says something about* the ideas of others.
6 He *says* his success *comes from* luck rather than hard work.

3 **Use three of the collocations from exercise 1 to write sentences about yourself.**

WRITING Describing a common fear

You are going to learn about developing paragraphs and using the present perfect. You are then going to use these to write a paragraph describing fear.

Writing skill

DEVELOPING PARAGRAPHS

When you write a paragraph, everything in the paragraph should be connected to one main idea. This main idea is usually given in a topic sentence, which is often the first sentence of a paragraph. All other details in the paragraph are there to support this main point. These supporting details are usually in the form of examples, explanations, or other specific information. The final sentence can contain an additional detail, example, or explanation, or it can be a concluding sentence. Sometimes it makes the transition to the topic of the next paragraph.

1   Look at the two paragraphs below. In the first one, the function of the sentences is marked. Do the same for the second paragraph.

Paragraph 1

topic sentence

specific information

When an immediate threat appears, our mind focuses on the things that are really important. The brain releases chemicals that make the mind more alert and active when attention is needed. If you know you are about to speak in front of 200 people, you are likely to be thinking about nothing else other than what you want to say. You are unlikely to be thinking about what you are going to have for dinner tonight.

example

Paragraph 2

Our response not only becomes faster, but another benefit of fear is that we also become stronger when we are faced with danger. Under pressure, skills such as putting a key in a door usually become worse, but physical skills such as running and jumping tend to improve. If an angry dog is chasing you, you are probably going to run faster. In a normal situation, we often only use 65% of our strength, but studies have shown that this can increase to as much as 85% in more dangerous situations.

2   Look at the following two paragraphs and write a topic sentence for each.

Paragraph 1

_____ Common symptoms associated with phobias include feeling dizzy, getting out of breath, feeling sick, and even a fear of dying. If these feelings are strong, they might lead to a panic attack. Phobias can even make some people isolate themselves from others, making it difficult for them to live a normal life.

Paragraph 2

_____ Adults teach children to fear some things before the child is presented with the situation, through their words or actions. Children may also notice the fears of adults in their family. If they see a parent scared by a situation, they are also likely to be scared by it. Fortunately, many children outgrow their phobias as they get older.

Grammar

THE PRESENT PERFECT SIMPLE

We use the present perfect to talk about events that happened at an unspecified point in time, or to connect the past with the present.

Form	Example
have/has + past participle	We can develop the fear after we **have seen** something that makes us scared.
	We **have developed** a response to situations that might cause us harm.

We use *since* to talk about *when* something started and *for* to talk about *how long* something has lasted.

Form	Example
present perfect + *since* + point in time	I'**ve been** scared of dogs **since** a dog bit me when I was five years old.
present perfect + *for* + length of time	I'**ve had** this phobia **for** 13 years.

In academic writing, the present perfect is also often used to report research findings.

Studies **have shown** *that this can increase to as much as 85% in more dangerous situations.*

1 **Complete these sentences with the present perfect form of the verb in parentheses.**

1 I _____ (be) afraid of flying since I was a child.

2 I _____ (hear) that flying is the most common fear.

3 I _____ (not feel) so scared since I was little.

4 I _____ (give) so many talks I'm no longer scared of public speaking.

5 _____ (you / have) the feeling of time moving slowly when you are scared?

6 _____ (you / see) a doctor about your fears?

2 **Write sentences using *for* and *since* to describe these people's fears.**

1 not fly / a child

   I haven't flown since I was a child.

2 take an elevator / five years

3 go to the dentist / ten years old

4 speak in public / two years

3 **Think about your fears and when they started. Write sentences explaining how long you have had the fear.**

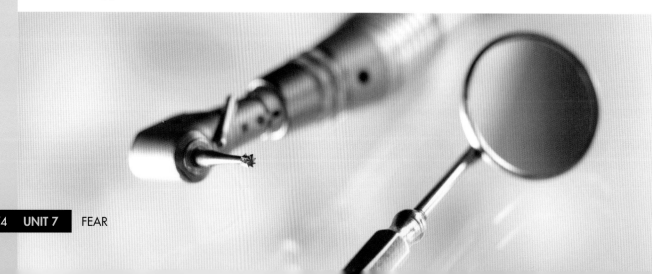

WRITING TASK

Write a paragraph describing a common fear.

BRAINSTORM

1 Read the paragraph below and <u>underline</u> the topic sentences. Highlight the supporting details. What types of supporting details are included: examples, explanations, or more information?

Have you ever felt afraid in an enclosed space like an elevator? You may have what is known as claustrophobia. This is a fear of being in a space you feel you cannot leave. If somebody with claustrophobia enters a small space like an elevator, they will probably panic when the doors close. Many situations, such as traveling in an elevator, subway train, or airplane, cause claustrophobic people to panic, but in the worst cases, even closing the door to a room can cause this feeling.

2 You are going to write a paragraph about a common fear. Think about fears you or other people have. Take notes.

PLAN

Plan your paragraph. Look back at your brainstorm and write a topic sentence. Decide how you want to organize your paragraph.

WRITE

Write a paragraph describing a common fear. Pay attention to your paragraph structure, especially the topic sentence and supporting details. Try to provide an example using a conditional sentence. Your paragraph should be 100–150 words long.

SHARE

Exchange paragraphs with a partner. Look at the checklist on page 109 and provide feedback to your partner.

REWRITE AND EDIT

Consider your partner's comments and rewrite your paragraph.

Ways of working with others

by Stella Cottrell

Supportive working

Talk through your difficulties and concerns—others may feel the same way. Help each other to find solutions.

Encourage

Let others know what they do well. Ask their opinions. If you appreciated a particular contribution, tell them!

Collaborate

Give each other suggestions about the best things to read for an assignment. Talk about what you have read. Share strategies for coping with work, children, money, projects.

Divide different aspects of your study between you. For example, you could each check a different library or organization for information, or you could take part in each other's project questionnaires.

Cooperate

Go through your lecture notes together and see if you picked out different points. Photocopy essays once they have been marked and read each other's. What differences do you notice?

Offer constructive criticism

If you disagree with another person's ideas and if the issue needs to be addressed, then phrase your suggestions in a positive way. Suggest ways forward for improvement, rather than criticizing what is wrong, or was wrong in the past.

- Offer criticism only if invited to do so.
- Point out what is good, as well as what could be improved.
- Comment on behavior or products, not on people.
- Be realistic—only suggest changes that can be achieved.
- Be selective—choose one or two items that would make a real difference.
- Be precise—give a clear example.
- Be sympathetic—use a voice and a manner that help others accept your criticism.

Receive criticism

- Listen attentively.
- Take time to think about what has been said. Look for the truth in it.
- Thank others for constructive comments.
- Ask questions to clarify anything you do not understand.

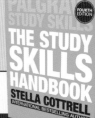

Hazards to watch out for

Beware of copying

All completed pieces of written work must be in your own words—so be careful that you don't appear to be copying other people and that they don't appear to be copying you.

Share work fairly

If you share tasks out, make sure it is on a fair basis. Consider what is fair in the circumstances, and what to do if someone really cannot do what they agreed to do.

Encourage others, but look after yourself

Encourage other people if they are having problems—but avoid being drawn into anybody else's depression or negativity.

Planning to prevent difficulties

If you are going to work with somebody else over a period of time, think through what you hope to gain from working together, and what hazards may arise. You could each write down your reflections under three headings:

- Advantages
- Potential difficulties
- Ways we could deal with these difficulties

Go through all the advantages together. Consider each potential difficulty and brainstorm ideas for ways of dealing with it. Be creative in looking for strategies. If you still can't think of a solution, speak to another friend, a tutor, or a student counselor.

Stories

READING	Fact and opinion
	Identifying reasons
VOCABULARY	Dictionary skills
WRITING	Definition paragraphs
GRAMMAR	Defining relative clauses

Discussion point

Discuss these questions with a partner.

1 Who are some of the most famous people or national heroes in your country? Are they writers, politicians, athletes …?

One of the most famous people is … He/She is a …
… is a national hero. He/She was …

2 What are the stories about these people? Does everyone believe these stories?

One well-known story about … is …
Most people believe this, but …

3 Why do you think the facts in stories sometimes get changed?

The facts can change because …

Vocabulary preview

Use the words in the box to complete the text.

biography	consciously	elaborates	myth	narrative	plot	protagonist	recall

A (1) _____, which is basically a (2) _____ telling the story of someone's life, often (3) _____ on the details of that story. But how accurate are biographies or even autobiographies when they rely on people to (4) _____ events from many years ago? Furthermore, people often (5) _____ change the details of a story to make it more interesting and engaging. Rather than telling the truth, a life story might become more like a (6)_____ with no real sense of accuracy. This can be especially true if a life story is being made into a movie—according to screenwriters the (7) _____ needs to be interesting and the audience need to develop feelings for the (8) _____, the main person in the story. The story we read or watch on the screen can be very different from reality.

READING 1 National hero

Before you read

Which of the following situations do you think would be the most heroic?

a A soccer player recovers from a serious injury to score the winning goal in a FIFA World Cup™ final.

b A firefighter risks her own life to help people injured in a car crash.

c A mountaineer climbs one of the tallest and most dangerous mountains in the world.

Global reading

> **FACT AND OPINION**
>
> A fact is something that is clearly true, but an opinion is something that some people believe, which might not be true. Below is some typical language used when a writer wants to indicate that information they are presenting is opinion rather than fact:
>
> *It is believed …   It is widely understood that …   People agree that …*

Read *National hero*. Which of these sentences are opinions and which are facts? How do you know? Discuss your answers with a partner.

1 Scott didn't plan to race to the South Pole.

2 Scott did not plan the trip well.

3 Robert Peary and Frederick Cook didn't reach the North Pole.

4 The failure of Scott's expedition was due to bad luck.

5 Scott's expedition brought back many items for scientists to study.

6 Scott's scientific aims stopped him being the first to the South Pole.

Close reading

Read *National hero* again and complete these sentences.

1 Many people went to Scott's _____.

2 There was a _____ to reach the poles.

3 People _____ their opinion of Scott in the 1970s.

4 Amundsen planned to go to the _____.

5 Amundsen's team were _____ than Scott's team.

1 When Robert Falcon Scott, or "Scott of the Antarctic" as he is commonly known, was reported dead, an elaborate funeral was held in London. The King of England attended, and thousands stood outside St Paul's Cathedral, far more people than had stood there after the *Titanic* sank just the year before. So why did so many people attend the funeral of just one explorer?

2 The early 1900s were a time of exploration. Most of the world had been mapped, but the polar regions were the last unknown places for people to explore. Scott first went to the Antarctic between 1901 and 1904, and then returned in 1910. Scott hadn't planned to be in the race to be the first person to reach the South Pole. He had simply planned another scientific trip in 1910, combined with an attempt to reach the South Pole. Unknown to him at first, a Norwegian named Roald Amundsen was trying to reach the Pole at the same time. Unfortunately, Scott lost the race to the Pole, and died on the journey back. His body was found in the Antarctic in a tent with some of his colleagues. The details of his final days were described in Scott's diaries.

3 Britain was going through a time of change in the early twentieth century. Its empire was in decline, and the roles of men and women were starting to change. Scott became a national hero who once again made Britain feel "great." This heroic image of Scott remained until a biography that destroyed the myth was published in the 1970s. The book showed that its protagonist and his team had made a number of major mistakes: not enough dogs, unprepared men who couldn't ski, and indecision. In the 1970s, Britain was again going through a difficult period, with unemployment increasing and the country in industrial decline. The nation had become more cynical and started to reflect on its past failures.

4 Scott wanted to be first to reach the Pole. However, he also planned to conduct research, so he took a team of scientists with him. It was an unexpected turn of events that made the expedition into a race—a situation that Scott hadn't consciously chosen. Amundsen hadn't planned to go to the South Pole; his ambition was to reach the North Pole. However, in 1909 two U.S. explorers—Robert Peary and Frederick Cook—announced that their two separate expeditions had reached the North Pole. Both claims were accepted at the time and backed by newspapers in the U.S. Today, however, neither of the explorers' stories is accepted as true because their proof of arrival was so poor and the speeds they claimed were unbelievably fast.

Scott's team

Roald Amundsen

5 The claims forced Amundsen to change his plan and aim instead to be the first to reach the South Pole. It was said that Amundsen's team were much better prepared than Scott's and that Scott made many mistakes. However, others believe Scott was actually unlucky with the weather, and he was more focused on the scientific aims of his expedition. Scott's expedition brought back 40,000 scientific specimens, including almost 20 kilograms of rock. Of the 2,000 animal and plant species the expedition brought back, some 400 were new discoveries. Some of the fossils also led scientists to develop the idea there was once one supercontinent that went on to break up. If Scott hadn't had these scientific aims, he might well have been the first person to reach the South Pole, and he might have lived to tell the tale.

NATIONAL HERO

Developing critical thinking

Discuss these questions in a group.

1 Explorers such as Scott do not often become heroes anymore. Today, many heroes are famous athletes, actors, or singers. Why do you think the idea of who is a hero changes over time?

Heroes have changed because ...

2 Do you know any other "heroes" whose reputation has changed over time? Why did these changes happen?

One person whose reputation has changed is ...

ACADEMIC KEYWORDS		
commonly	(adv)	/ˈkɑmənli/
reflect	(v)	/rɪˈflekt/
separate	(adj)	/ˈsepərət/

READING 2 Mixed memories

Before you read

1 Read a mother's and her child's memories of the same event. What differences are there?

> He was really scared and kept crying all the time. He wouldn't talk to the other children and cried every time his teacher spoke to him. His teacher couldn't understand why he was always so upset.

> I was a little nervous and scared but really excited. I made lots of friends and really liked my teacher. It was one of the best days of my life.

He remembers ... but she says ...

2 Discuss with a partner why you think there are big differences in the memories of the mother and her son in exercise 1.

He remembers things differently because ...

Global reading

1 Skim *Mixed memories* and decide on the best heading (1–3).

  1 How to write a biography

  2 Why we forget things

  3 How life stories are created

2 Read *Mixed memories* again and match the summaries a–f with paragraphs 2–7.

  a The events in early adulthood are the most important in shaping who we become.

  b Childhood relationships shape our way of thinking and our ability to tell stories.

  c Young adults' most important memories change constantly, depending on what is happening in their lives, whereas older people's memories are more fixed.

  d As teenagers, our storytelling is more imaginative than at any other time.

  e We edit the stories of our lives to give them logic and often to make them seem more positive.

  f Good memories usually last the longest, and we can choose to forget bad memories.

Close reading

IDENTIFYING REASONS

Reasons for an event or situation are often given in a text to further explain or support a main idea. It is important to identify these as they will give you an understanding of why something occurs. There are certain standard phrases that highlight reasons, for example:

because, due to, hence, on account of, as a result.

They are also commonly signaled by referring to studies that support or explain the reason for something. For example:

Studies have shown that …

Studies have found …

Look at *Mixed memories* and find reasons for these situations or events.

1 Some children tell positive stories.

2 Some children remember more detail.

3 Teenagers constantly replay new experiences in their mind.

4 Our important memories change a lot in our early twenties.

5 Our longest memories are usually positive.

6 We continually rewrite our life stories.

M I X E D   M E M O R I E S

1 Since many people now live such long and often complicated lives, it is perhaps not surprising that we try to remember and organize them into a coherent story. But how are our life stories shaped and just how accurate are the biographical details that we all recall?

2 We start to build the plot of our life story from the moment we are born. Recent research has shown that children who are close to their parents and enjoy strong family relationships will look back on their lives as being positive. Their story will have a happy plot. On the other hand, those who lack a close relationship with family often tell a more pessimistic story about key life events. It has also been found that parents have a strong impact on their children's ability to remember and retell details of their life. The more time a parent spends reading to a child, the better the child will become at storytelling.

3 Our storytelling reaches its most creative stage in our early teenage years. Many teenagers talk about life events as if they are the heroic protagonist. Even very mundane stories are elaborated on to take on an almost mythical status. By the late teenage years, the stories start to become more realistic, but are still important in shaping how we see our lives.

4 Late teenage years and early adulthood are full of so many firsts that it is impossible for them not to be key parts of our life story. Because these events are so significant and the memories of them are so strong, we frequently replay them in our minds. This constant conscious reviewing and replaying goes a long way to shaping who we become in later life.

5 Psychologist David Rubin has defined something that he calls "a memory bump." This refers to the idea that middle-aged and older adults remember most strongly things that happened between the ages of ten and 30. This group is significantly different from adults in their early twenties, when important memories change constantly. In his study, Rubin asked college students to tell him their most important memories. When asked the same question six months later, only 12% of the college students repeated the same story. When we are so young, we are still writing our own life story, and there are often many major changes, such as our first job, marriage, and children. As a result, the relative importance of events in our lives is always changing.

6 Our longest-lasting memories are mainly positive ones, because we tell these stories most frequently to other people. As a result of this repetition, they take on more and more importance. Studies have shown that people can choose to forget certain memories, which could explain why we sometimes don't remember sad or unpleasant events.

7 Wherever we are from and whatever our life story is, we tend to continually rewrite it. We create stories to give logic to our lives. If we choose a certain career, we often look back on our past and try to find a significant event that made us take that career path. We also tend to add details to our narrative to make good things even better. So are we living a lie or does this tendency allow us to be more optimistic and go forward in life?

HOME   NEWS   **STORIES**   MESSAGE BOARD

ACADEMIC KEYWORDS		
logic	(n)	/ˈlɑdʒɪk/
relative	(adj)	/ˈrelətɪv/
tendency	(n)	/ˈtendənsi/

Developing critical thinking

1 Discuss these questions in a group.

1 Do you agree that past events and how we view them shape who we become in the future?

I think past events shape / don't shape us because ...

2 Why do you think people focus on positive rather than negative memories?

We tend to focus on positive memories because ...

2 Think about the ideas from *National hero* and *Mixed memories* and discuss these questions in a group.

1 Why do we rewrite the stories of famous people in history? Is it for the same reasons we rewrite our own life stories?

The reasons are/aren't the same ...
It is/isn't the same because ...

2 When talking about the past, how can you change how a situation is portrayed?

The main factors are ...

Vocabulary skill

DICTIONARY SKILLS

While it is often easier to simply translate a word from a text using a bilingual dictionary, doing this does not really help you to learn the word. Translating isn't an active process, so it may mean you forget the meaning of the new words you have looked up. By learning to use a monolingual dictionary effectively, you can enhance your vocabulary learning skills. It is also important to pay attention to the context of the word within a text when you are dealing with multimeaning words.

1 Read the definition of the word *conduct* from the *Macmillan English Dictionary* and complete the information.

a _____ tells you how to pronounce the word.

b _____ shows the frequency of the word.

c _____ means it is usually used with a direct object.

conduct /kənˈdʌkt/

 VERB ★★★

[T] [OFTEN PASSIVE] to do something in an organized way. In ordinary speech it is more usual to say that someone carries something out

2 Many words have multiple meanings. Use your dictionary to help decide the meaning of each word in the pairs of sentences.

1 a The organization was denied legal *status*.
  b The job brings with it *status* and a high income.
2 a They were traveling at a *constant* speed.
  b This entrance is in *constant* use.
3 a He *claims* it is true.
  b She finally *claimed* a place on the winning team.
4 a His generation firmly believed they could *shape* the future.
  b He *shaped* it into a ball.
5 a The game *lasts* 80 minutes.
  b I won't *last* much longer if I don't eat soon.

WRITING Describing a study subject

You are going to learn about defining paragraphs and defining relative clauses. You are then going to use these to write a paragraph defining a subject you study or want to study.

Writing skill

DEFINITION PARAGRAPHS

In academic writing, it is important to define any key terms clearly, especially when the definition isn't agreed upon or there are multiple meanings of a word. You may also need to provide definitions for difficult or confusing terms. In essays, definitions are often expanded into a paragraph to help make it clear to the reader what you mean. Typical ways of extending definitions are the following: to give examples, to give further details, to move from general to specific, and to discuss the advantages and disadvantages of the thing being defined.

1 Look at the paragraph below and label each of the features in the box.

definition   example   further details   ~~topic sentence~~

One way of defining people, which was used by psychologists in the past, was to divide people into pessimists and optimists. A pessimist is someone who takes a negative approach to life, while an optimist is someone who approaches life positively. For instance, a pessimist would view a glass as half empty, while an optimist would see a glass as half full. From a psychological perspective, optimists would believe that they have control over their own life and destiny, while pessimists would feel that they had no control over their own destiny.

Topic sentence

2 Look at the sections of a paragraph defining psychology. Number the sentences in the correct order.

☐ It looks at how people behave and react in certain situations, and the underlying reasons for such outcomes.

☐ Psychology is a subject which involves the study of the behavior of humans and animals.

☐ While this stereotypical scenario is common in psychology, it extends much further into the field of biology than many people realize.

☐ For instance, it may analyze the events of someone's childhood and their impact on their behavior in later life.

Grammar

DEFINING RELATIVE CLAUSES

A relative clause describes a thing or person. One type of relative clause is a defining relative clause. A defining relative clause gives information to explain the specific one or the specific group the writer means. It gives essential information about the thing or the person the writer is describing.

Sentence	Meaning
Students are successful after their degree.	All students are successful after their degree.
defining relative clause *Students **who work hard** are successful after their degree.*	Only the students who work hard are successful, not all students.

A relative clause begins with a relative pronoun. The relative pronoun used is different depending on what is being described.

who = person   *which/that* = thing   *where* = place
why = reason   *when* = time   *whose* = possessive

1 Complete these sentences with *whose, when, where,* or *why*.

1 Children _____ parents read to them are likely to have a better imagination.

2 The town _____ I lived as a teenager holds some of my strongest memories.

3 Locations _____ expeditions take place are often remote and unexplored.

4 The reason _____ we forget negative memories seems obvious.

5 The reason _____ Scott took five people to the South Pole, and not four, is not clear.

6 The time _____ Scott died in the Antarctic was the coldest on record.

7 People _____ memories are affected by age often tell a limited range of stories.

2 Complete these sentences using *whose, when, where,* or *why* and your own ideas.

1 The person _____ achievements I most admire is …

2 The reason _____ … is my strongest memory is …

3 The place _____ most of my memories were formed is …

4 The time _____ I was happiest was …

WRITING TASK

Write a paragraph describing an academic subject you would like to study.

BRAINSTORM

1 Read the paragraph below. What is the main topic? What is being defined? <u>Underline</u> the defining relative clause.

Stories play a central role in the representation of all societies around the world. In particular, stories that have a moral show what is considered right and wrong in a society. In European culture, Aesop's fables are a classic example of this literary form. These fables demonstrate, for example, that lying, impatience, and greed are negative qualities.

2 You are going to write a paragraph defining a subject you study or want to study. Think about what it is and what is involved in the study of the subject. Write notes in the table below.

What the subject is	What is involved

PLAN

Plan your paragraph. Look back at your notes from the brainstorm section and write a definition of your subject, using a relative clause. Think about the supporting detail you can add.

WRITE

Write a paragraph describing the subject. Pay attention to your organization and use of relative clauses. Your paragraph should be 100–150 words long.

SHARE

Exchange paragraphs with a partner. Look at the checklist on page 109 and provide feedback to your partner.

REWRITE AND EDIT

Consider your partner's comments and rewrite your paragraph.

STUDY SKILLS Reviewing material

Getting started

Discuss these questions with a partner.

1 Do you feel confident taking exams? Why or why not?
2 How long before an exam do you think you should review material? Should you only review material to prepare for exams?
3 How do you review material from a course?

Scenario

Read this scenario and think about what Manuel did right and what he did wrong.

Consider it

Read the tips about reviewing material. Discuss each one with a partner. Which ones do you do and why? Which do you think you might use in future?

1 **Focus your notes** Don't make extensive notes on everything you read. Try to focus on and prioritize key topics.
2 **Organize your notes** It will be easier to review the material from your course if your notes are clear and well organized—for example you should use lots of colors, pictures, and diagrams to highlight key points. Go over this work on a regular basis and begin intense revision four weeks before any exam.
3 **Work with others** Doing revision sessions with friends can be good for motivation. It gives you the opportunity to test each other and learn from each other.
4 **Use revision cards** They can be used to record important facts, dates, names, and definitions.
5 **Use key word triggers** Use rhythms, pictures, sounds, and images to help remember key words.
6 **Record yourself** Some people remember well from listening and speaking. Try to record yourself and see if it works well for you.
7 **Use past exam papers** It's important when reviewing material to think about how you will have to use this knowledge. You can do this by looking at previous papers and looking at the question types.

Over to you

Discuss these questions with a partner.

1 How do your review techniques change as you get closer to the exam?
2 Who do you ask for help when reviewing a topic?
3 What subjects have you been most successful in? How did you prepare for these tests?

Manuel went to every single class in the first semester and took a lot of notes in lectures. He filed these notes in different course folders and read through them after class. He also read through the relevant chapters of the book each week and made long notes. Some of his friends liked to work together but he was sure he was the strongest student and he didn't want to share his knowledge with others. Manuel recorded key terms, dates, and names on small cards and regularly tested his memory of them. He also liked to use pictures and sounds to help him remember important information. When it was nearly time for the exam, Manuel practiced some of the past papers. This showed him where there were gaps in his knowledge, so he went back to his notes from lectures and from his reading. It was difficult to find the information he needed because the notes were so long and unfocused. He also found it difficult to think of different points of view on certain topics and wished he had discussed them more with his classmates.

READING	Reading charts and graphs
	Finding supporting evidence for main ideas
VOCABULARY	Cause and effect
WRITING	Using statistics
GRAMMAR	The passive: present and past perfect

Discussion point

Discuss these questions with a partner.

1 Where does your drinking water come from? Do you drink tap water or buy bottled water? Why?

   I usually drink ... because ...   It comes from ...

2 Water covers more than 70% of the Earth's surface, yet many parts of the world don't have enough drinking water. Why is this?

   Most of the water is ...   There isn't enough water in ... because ...

3 Which of the following water-related problems do you think is the most serious? Why?

   drought   flooding   water pollution

Vocabulary preview

Complete the sentences with the words in the box.

| concede | deprived | desperate | forecast | originated | simulation |

1 Wind power _____ in Persia over 1,000 years ago.
2 It was a _____ situation—there was hardly any water left.
3 When developing a new design, engineers often use a computer _____ to test whether it will work before building it.
4 Engineers sometimes have to _____ defeat when things don't work.
5 The company has _____ that it will sell four million bottles.
6 As a result of the flood, residents of the area were _____ of electricity, clean water, and fresh food for three weeks.

READING 1 Fresh water delivery

Before you read

Look at these potential solutions to water shortages. Rank them in order of the most effective to least effective (1 = most effective).

| build reservoirs | drink salt water |
| persuade people to use less water | transport ice from the polar regions |

Global reading

Read *Fresh water delivery* and complete the notes on each paragraph below.

1 *1.1 bn ppl—no clean drinking water. Fresh water in glaciers & icebergs.*

2 _____

3 *Iceberg towing—old idea—1800s. Isaacs' plan—tow iceberg for dr. water in 1950s.*

4 _____

5 *Mougin relaunched project using simulations.*

6 _____

7 _____

Close reading

READING CHARTS AND GRAPHS

Visuals can help you understand a text since their titles often highlight key themes. The information presented often provides supporting detail.

After you read a text, try to make connections between the information in the chart and the information in the text.

Answer the questions about the charts below.

1 Is most of the water on Earth ☐ salt water or ☐ fresh water? (check one)
2 How much of the water on our planet is seawater? ___ (%)
3 How much of the Earth's fresh water is easy to access? ___ (%)
4 How much of it is frozen? more than ___ (fraction)
5 How much does it cost per person per day to desalinate water? ___

1 There are 1.1 billion people on Earth who live without access to clean drinking water. At the same time, trillions of gallons of fresh water a year disappear into the ocean, useless to these water-deprived areas. While the polar ice caps are made of undrinkable frozen seawater, icebergs that break off from glaciers are tremendous stores of fresh water. In fact, it's estimated that more than two-thirds of the Earth's fresh water is in the form of ice. In a recent five-year period, an average of 195 cubic kilometers of ice fell from glaciers in Greenland, annually. That equals 51 trillion gallons of potential drinking water each year.

2 Desperate times call for desperate measures. To find solutions to these water shortages, a French engineer is working on an extraordinary idea: drag massive icebergs from the polar regions to dry areas that are desperate for water, and melt them for drinking water.

3 The idea of towing icebergs from the poles is not a new one. According to the Encyclopedia of Antarctica, in the mid to late 1800s small icebergs were towed up the coast of southern Chile to use for refrigeration. In the 1950s, John Isaacs turned the idea into a highly-ambitious scheme for providing fresh drinking water. One of his proposals was to find an eight-billion ton iceberg in the Antarctic and tow it to San Clemente Island near California in just 200 days. According to Isaacs, it would take much less energy to tow it there than it would to desalinate it. This idea remained popular in the late twentieth century but was never actually carried out.

4 Perhaps the person most likely to make the idea a reality is Georges Mougin, a Frenchman who has spent the past 30 years working on it. In 1975, a Saudi prince challenged Mougin to bring an iceberg from the North Pole to the Red Sea. The project failed because the cost would have been huge ($100 million), but Mougin didn't concede defeat.

5 After many more setbacks, Mougin partnered with a French company that specializes in creating 3-D simulations. He relaunched the project as IceDream and now uses the advanced forecasting technology to help predict ocean currents and other variables, such as wind, which could cause problems for a possible ocean crossing.

6 Mougin's team of glaciologists and engineers are working toward IceDream's first goal: drag a single iceberg from the coast of Canada across the Atlantic. To be successful, they need to find the right kind of iceberg (flat and table-shaped rather than a towering mountain-shaped one), surround it with a gigantic "skirt," and tow it across the ocean before it melts.

7 But even if it worked, would it be cost effective? We can compare the costs to another extreme method of getting fresh water for dry areas—desalination. This is the process of removing the salt from sea water to make it drinkable. This method certainly isn't cheap: a recently-constructed plant in Saudi Arabia cost $3.8 billion to build—and in addition there are high running costs. So how do these costs compare to towing an iceberg? It has been estimated that it would cost $11.5 million to tow an iceberg big enough to supply 35,000 people with water for a year. Certainly cheaper than building a desalination plant, but it would provide water for far fewer people. Estimates suggest that water from towing an iceberg would cost more than three times as much as desalinated water. So unless Georges Mougin can come up with a much cheaper way to transport icebergs, his dream may never be realized.

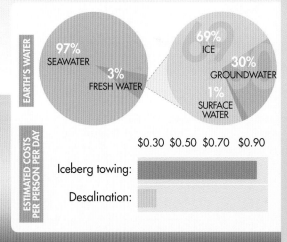

FRESH WATER
DELIVERY

Developing critical thinking

Discuss these questions in a group.

1 Do you think that towing icebergs is a good idea? Is the high cost of transporting icebergs worth the fresh water they could provide? Explain.

It is/isn't worth the cost because ...

2 Do you think finding an alternative source is the solution to the world's fresh water shortage, or do people just need to be more careful in their use of water?

Finding an alternative source ...   People need to ...

ACADEMIC KEYWORDS		
compare	(v)	/kəm'peər/
single	(adj)	/'sɪŋg(ə)l/
supply	(v)	/sə'plaɪ/

READING 2 The world's largest garbage dump

Before you read

Discuss these questions with a partner.

1 Which of the following do you recycle at home?

I usually recycle ... but it's difficult to recycle ... where I live.

2 Where does trash go if it's not recycled?

It largely goes ...

3 Aside from recycling, what should people be doing to reduce the amount of plastic waste?

RECYCLABLE MATERIALS/OBJECTS	
bottles	paper
cardboard	plastic bottles
glass	plastic packaging

Global reading

Scan *The world's largest garbage dump* and complete these sentences.

1 The garbage patch is located in the _____ Ocean.

2 Most of the debris comes from sources on _____.

3 The garbage patch was formed by _____.

4 Marine debris has been shown to _____ ocean animals.

Close reading

FINDING SUPPORTING EVIDENCE FOR MAIN IDEAS

Factual texts often include evidence in the form of examples and statistics to support the main ideas. You will sometimes be asked to present this evidence in discussions, presentations, or when writing about a topic.

1 **Match the main ideas with the supporting evidence in the table below.**

Main ideas	Supporting evidence
1 Marine debris can harm ocean life.	a A fish caught by Moore's research boat had _____ pieces of plastic in its stomach.
2 The amount of plastic in the patch is increasing.	b Recent water samples contained twice as much plastic as _____ years ago.
3 The garbage patch may have an active, healthy ecosystem.	c According to experts, _____% of the trash comes from sources on land and _____% originates from ships at sea.
4 There is a huge amount of trash in the garbage patch.	d A large amount of _____, phytoplankton, and zooplankton have been found in one of the areas, and _____ have multiplied.
5 Only a small proportion of the trash comes from ships.	e The garbage patch contains more than _____ tons of trash.
6 The trash in the water may be poisoning food eaten by humans.	f Hydrocarbons and the pesticide DDT enter the _____.

2 **Read *The world's largest garbage dump* again and complete the blanks in the supporting evidence.**

The world's largest
GARBAGE DUMP

When we think of an island in the Pacific Ocean, we might think of palm trees, a warm sun, and soft ocean breezes. But you may be surprised to discover that there is an enormous "island" of floating garbage, more than twice the size of France, somewhere between California and Japan. This moving patch of trash is the largest garbage dump on the planet.

In fact, the Great Pacific Garbage Patch is more like a "plastic soup" than an island—it can't be seen in satellite images, as it is made of small pieces, and much of it is below the surface of the water. It has been estimated that this colossal patch of garbage contains more than 3.5 million tons of debris, much of it plastic. Researchers have noted that the patch has doubled in size every decade and forecast that this trend will continue. Moreover, it is not the only such garbage patch in the world's oceans: scientists have used their knowledge of currents to predict that there are at least four others.

So where does all the trash originate? Experts believe that 80% comes from sources on land and 20% comes from trash thrown out by ships at sea. The garbage patch itself was formed by ocean currents. A high-pressure zone of air called the North Pacific Subtropical Gyre forces ocean surface currents to move in a slow clockwise pattern, creating a giant whirlpool that sucks garbage from other parts of the ocean into the patch.

The garbage patch was discovered in 1997 by an American, Charles Moore, who was sailing home from a boat race in Hawaii. He was a wealthy businessman at the time, but as a result of this experience, he sold his business interests and became an environmental activist. Ever since, his time and financial resources have been dedicated to studying the garbage patch and publicizing the harmful effects of disposable plastics.

His foundation takes water samples from the patch and analyzes them for the amount of plastic and toxic chemicals. Fish caught in the research boat's nets have also been tested. The samples have shown that the plastic in the patch and the Pacific Ocean in general is increasing. Water samples taken recently contained twice as much plastic as samples from ten years before.

How harmful is it? It has been shown that marine debris can entangle or otherwise harm ocean life. For example, animals may eat the garbage, which not only damages their stomachs but can also make them feel full so that they stop eating the food they need to survive. One recent catch from Moore's research boat had 84 pieces of plastic in its stomach. Because the garbage patch moves, trash has also been swept onto land, endangering shore animals such as seals. Dr. Eriksen, a U.S. researcher, believes that the trash-filled water also poses a risk to human health. The tiny plastic pieces attract man-made chemicals such as hydrocarbons and DDT, a toxic substance used to kill insects. Fish eat this contaminated plastic and we eat the fish. "What goes into the ocean goes into these animals and onto your dinner plate. It's that simple," said Dr. Eriksen.

It had been suggested by several scientists that the garbage patch actually has an active, healthy ecosystem after one of the floating areas had been found to have a large amount of fish, phytoplankton, and zooplankton. It has been noted that, with so much trash to float on, some species such as crabs grow to be more abundant than they would without the plastic debris. However, it is believed that many of these garbage-dwellers may be invasive species, or that they might alter the natural food chain and deprive other species of food. Crabs which usually live on floating wood in the open ocean have adapted to living on the plastic in the garbage patch and multiplied as a result. Their potential impact on the ecosystem has not yet been determined.

While researchers continue to study the garbage patch and its effects on ocean life, an observer might ask: why are we studying it and not actually cleaning it up? There is no doubt that it would be an expensive and difficult clean-up operation. As it is so far from land, transporting the necessary equipment would require a huge amount of fuel, creating massive carbon emissions. Because much of the trash is broken into tiny pieces, it would also be very difficult to collect. And even if we could extract it, what then? Project Kaisei, a Japanese project which aims to clean up the garbage patch, suggests turning the trash into fuel to burn; however, this would then pollute the atmosphere. Arguably, any potential solution risks causing further environmental damage.

Instead of trying to clean up the patch, perhaps conservation organizations should focus on changing people's behavior. If we all throw away less plastic, we can stop the patch from getting bigger.

Developing critical thinking

1 Discuss these questions in a group.

1 How serious a problem do you think the Great Pacific Garbage Patch is? Why?

2 Who is responsible for cleaning up or limiting the impact of an environmental mess like the Great Pacific Garbage Patch? Why?

It's the responsibility of ... because ...

ACADEMIC KEYWORDS		
alter	(v)	/ˈɔltər/
operation	(n)	/ˌɑpəˈreɪʃ(ə)n/
solution	(n)	/səˈluʃ(ə)n/

2 Think about the ideas from *Fresh water delivery* and *The world's largest garbage dump* and discuss these questions in a group.

1 Is it more important to deal with the impact man has already had on our planet, or to change current human behavior? Why?

2 Which do you think is a bigger concern: pollution or water shortages?

I am more concerned about ... because ...

Vocabulary skill

CAUSE AND EFFECT

Form	Examples
<u>Nouns</u> *origin, consequence, impact, relationship, influence, reason*	*Fish numbers have declined dramatically as a **consequence** of overfishing.*
<u>Verbs</u> *affect, associate with, contribute to, result in, lead to, produce*	*The growth of the world's population has **led to** greater demand for resources.*
<u>Conjunctions used to connect clauses</u> *as, because, if, since, so*	*The situation has gotten much worse **because** man has become so dependent on fossil fuels.*
<u>Words and phrases used to connect sentences</u> *as a result, consequently, hence, therefore, thus*	*The plastic dump is particularly good for crabs to live on. **As a result**, their populations are growing.*

1 Match the two halves of the sentences 1–4 to a–d

1 Carbon dioxide pollution has contributed to … ____

2 There are over one billion people without access to clean drinking water. ____

3 Many desalination plants are currently powered by oil and the result is … ____

4 The increased consumption of bottled water has contributed to … ____

a Consequently, scientists are exploring numerous ways to increase fresh water supplies.

b changes in marine ecosystems.

c the increased amounts of plastic in the ecosystem.

d that the price of water has become dependent on the price of oil in some places.

2 Complete these sentences with the expressions in the box.

as	as a result	cause of	one effect	result in

1 High levels of consumption of plastics can _____ wider marine pollution.

2 Increased levels of pesticides is one _____ marine pollution.

3 Urban populations place greater pressure on water sources in certain areas. _____, the water supply is often unevenly distributed within a country.

4 _____ people's lifestyles have become more sedentary, they have consumed more goods.

5 _____ of towing icebergs might be to change ocean temperatures worldwide.

WRITING Writing about a water issue

You are going to learn about using statistics in your writing and using the passive. You are then going to use these to write a factual pamphlet about a water issue.

Writing skill

USING STATISTICS

When writing in certain subject areas such as science, business, and economics, using statistics supports your ideas and makes them stronger. While you are researching a topic, make a note of any statistics that support your main points. Choose the strongest ones and use them as supporting details in your article. If some of the points are related, you can organize them into a chart or graph.

1 Complete the article with these supporting statistics (a–e).

a It has been found that an average sized cruise ship produces around 1 million gallons of wastewater in one week.

b studies have shown that 80% of marine debris is plastic.

c The world's oceans have absorbed 40% of the carbon dioxide emissions produced by humans in the industrial age.

d In one recent year, our oceans suffered one major oil spill and seven medium-sized oil spills.

e approximately 80% of ocean pollution has been caused by people on land.

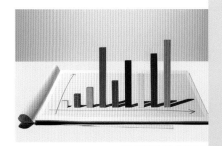

We cannot create new water.

For millions of years, the water we use today has been recycled over and over by natural cycles that clean the water after we use it. But those natural cycles are no longer sufficient to clean all the waste that humans put into it, and our water has become polluted.

Man is polluting all water systems but of particular concern is the pollution of our oceans. We are polluting the ocean in a number of ways, but the main pollutants are toxic waste, garbage, oil, and carbon dioxide from land sources. In fact, ____

In addition to the impact from land on ocean pollution another 20% of pollution is from ocean-based activity. Large boats carrying oil are responsible for much of the waste. Oil spills are the greatest culprit. ____ Cruise ships are also big polluters.

____

Garbage dumping, both from ships and from land, is another major cause of ocean pollution. One type of garbage is a particularly big problem: ____
Plastic waste suffocates fish and other sea animals such as whales, seals, dolphins, and penguins.

Finally, other human activities, such as the burning of fossil fuels, are also polluting our oceans. The carbon dioxide emitted not only pollutes the air but ultimately enters the ocean's ecosystem. ____ These are changing the chemistry of the oceans and killing coral reefs.

Changes clearly need to be made as soon as possible to limit our impact on the delicate ecosystems of the world's oceans.

2 Make a note of some statistics from *Fresh water delivery* or *The world's largest garbage dump*. Write a short paragraph using the statistics to support your ideas.

Grammar

THE PASSIVE: PRESENT AND PAST PERFECT

The passive is used to focus on the person or thing being acted upon and not the person or people doing the action. Writers also use the passive to give more importance to the action itself.

Form	Example
Present perfect passive *have/has + been + past participle*	*The impact of the program **has not yet been determined**.*
Past perfect passive *had + been + past participle*	*Before the program began, millions of bottles **had been thrown away** daily.*

Compare the sentences above with these active sentences:

Scientists have not yet determined the impact of the program.

Before the program began, people had thrown away millions of bottles daily.

1 Look at the sentences below. Which ones contain mistakes?

   1   Scientists have been analyzed the cause of the pollution.
   2   A variety of possible solutions had been investigated prior to the implementation of the current one.
   3   The long term consequences have not yet discovered.
   4   Studies showed that 20% of the trash had been thrown from ships.
   5   Environmentalists have long campaigned for change.

2 Work with a partner. Read these sentences and discuss why the passive was used.

   1   It <u>has long been known</u> that plastic pollution is dangerous to sea animals.
   2   The seawater in the area <u>had been tested</u> repeatedly by scientists studying the effect of ocean currents on pollution.
   3   Many attempts to transport an iceberg <u>had been made</u> before one engineer found a successful method.
   4   The possible impacts on the food chain <u>have been investigated</u>.
   5   The consumption of pesticides <u>has been linked</u> to increases in allergies.

3 Rewrite these sentences in the passive form. Omit the original subjects if they are unnecessary.

   1   Marine scientists have not yet found an economical way to harvest fresh water from icebergs.

   An economical way to harvest fresh water from icebergs has not yet been found.

   2   Campaigners have used various tactics to raise the public's awareness of the issue.

   _____

   3   Researchers have found growing populations of crabs in the area.

   _____

   4   Scientists had not known the effects prior to the study.

   _____

WRITING TASK

Write a persuasive pamphlet using evidence and statistics.

BRAINSTORM

1 You work for an environmental charity, and you are going to write a persuasive pamphlet for a campaign on one of these topics:
- why we need to save water
- why we need to use less disposable plastic.

Work with a partner and decide which of the topics you would like to write about.

2 Think about the points you want to make and add them to the table below. Read *Fresh water delivery* or *The world's largest garbage dump* again and try to find supporting evidence and statistics.

Points I want to make	Supporting evidence/statistics

PLAN

Look back at your brainstorm and decide on the order in which you are going to present your points. Which points are connected?

WRITE

Write a pamphlet about a water issue. Pay attention to your use of the passive. Be sure to use a variety of statistics to support your ideas.

SHARE

Exchange pamphlets with a partner. Look at the checklist on page 109 and provide feedback to your partner. Use a dictionary to look up any words you don't know. Your pamphlet should be 150–200 words long.

REWRITE AND EDIT

Consider your partner's comments and rewrite your pamphlet.

STUDY SKILLS Forming a study group

Getting started

Discuss these questions with a partner.

1 How, when, and where do you best like to study?
2 What do you find hardest about motivating yourself to study?
3 Do you ever study with a group of people?

Scenario

Read this scenario and think about what Lujain did right and what she did wrong.

Consider it

Read the tips about forming a study group. Discuss each one with a partner. Try to rank them in order of importance for forming a study group and then compare them with a partner.

1 **Listen to others** For a group to be effective, everyone should have a chance to express themselves. You may learn something from another student so try to encourage quieter students to participate. For example, refer to something another student said earlier, ask questions, and use positive body language.

2 **Create a supportive group** Remember that people have feelings. Try to make any criticisms of others constructive. It's not a competition to see who knows the most.

3 **Focus the meetings** Try to set an agenda for each meeting so that you stay focused and cover all the topics you need to study.

4 **Manage discussions** Groups can become ineffective if one person dominates. Try to encourage everyone to take part and use your agenda to remind you when to move on to a different topic.

5 **Share tasks** To reduce your workload, allocate different work to each person. Share out background reading or the reviewing of lectures. Then take turns to summarize what you learned for the rest of the group.

6 **Test your knowledge** At the end of each topic, ask everyone in the group to write one question on the topic, then ask the question to the person sitting on their left.

Over to you

Discuss these questions with a partner.

1 Why do you think it is important to vary study methods?
2 What are the advantages and disadvantages of studying in a group?
3 What do you think is the ideal number of students in a study group?

Lujain started to work in a study group before her exams because she was finding it difficult to motivate herself to study alone. The group met twice a week to cover all the topics before the exam. Lujain knew she was the strongest student in the group, so she helped the other students a lot. She was sure they all liked her helping them. However, she started to feel frustrated because she felt like she was their teacher. At first, the other students were quiet, but then after a week one of the others argued with her. Lujain won the argument and could tell the other students thought she was really clever. At the next meeting, no one else turned up, so Lujain studied on her own. When she was walking home, she was surprised to see her study group sitting together in a café laughing and looking happy.

READING	Identifying types of supporting details
	Bridge sentences
VOCABULARY	Finding meaning from synonyms or antonyms
WRITING	Presenting a claim
GRAMMAR	Indirect quotation

Discussion point

Discuss these questions with a partner.

1 Think of a person who is good at influencing others. What makes this person so persuasive?

... is really persuasive because ...

2 Which of these things do you think is easiest to do?

> to persuade someone that your opinion is right
> to persuade someone to buy something
> to persuade someone to feel better when they are sick

It's easiest to persuade people to ...   *It's not easy to convince people ...*

3 How do people and companies persuade us to buy things? Have you been persuaded to buy anything recently?

Companies try to persuade people by ...   *The last time I was persuaded to buy something ...*

Vocabulary preview

Match the words in bold with their definitions.

1 When she laughs, we can't stop ourselves from laughing, too—it's **infectious**.
2 He's very energetic and uses a lot of **gestures** when he speaks.
3 She has real **presence** when she enters the room.
4 She gave her presentation so **articulately** that very few questions were asked.

a an impressive appearance, or way of behaving and speaking
b movements, especially of the hands or head, that express meaning
c clearly and fluently
d likely to spread or influence others rapidly

5 The service award will greatly **enhance** our company's reputation.
6 **Stimulants** like coffee can prevent you from sleeping.
7 When I'm **drowsy**, I can't concentrate, and I just want to take a nap!
8 All the **trials** showed that the drug was not effective.

e tests of the performance or quality of something
f improve
g substances or medicines that make you feel more awake
h sleepy

READING 1 Charisma

Before you read

1 **Charisma is defined as "a strong personal quality that makes other people like and admire you." Who would you describe as having charisma? Why?**

... has charisma because ...

2 **Check (✓) the words you would associate with a charismatic person.**

☐ artificial ☐ independent
☐ confident ☐ leader
☐ enthusiastic ☐ nervous
☐ fascinating ☐ persuasive
☐ follower ☐ relaxed

Global reading

Skim *Charisma*. Match the paragraphs with their functions.

1 Paragraph 1 ___   a gives examples of how charisma can be learned
2 Paragraph 2 ___   b warns against trying to fake charisma
3 Paragraph 3 ___   c introduces the topic of charisma
4 Paragraph 4 ___   d explains how charismatic people affect others
5 Paragraph 5 ___   e defines charisma

Mahatma Gandhi

Winston Churchill

Napoleon Bonaparte

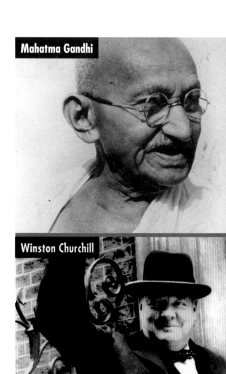

Close reading

IDENTIFYING TYPES OF SUPPORTING DETAILS

Writers use supporting details to support the main ideas of a text. Some types of support include the writer's own personal opinions, opinions from experts, logical explanations, statistics, and examples.

Read *Charisma* and look at the sentences below. Mark each one *S* for statistics, *E* for example, *EX* for explanation, *EO* for expert opinion, or *PO* for personal opinion. Not all the types appear here, and some appear more than once.

1 Richard Wiseman, a prominent psychologist, points out there are three key attributes of a charismatic person.

2 These skills allow charismatic people to affect and influence others at a deep emotional level.

3 For example, if you stand up straight and raise your chest, you are more likely to feel confident and inspire others to feel confidence in you.

4 Another expert says that the most charismatic people are good listeners.

5 One successful leadership coach points out that people pick up on that right away.

ACADEMIC KEYWORDS

affect	(v)	/əˈfekt/
personality	(n)	/ˌpɜrsəˈnæləti/
type	(n)	/taɪp/

CHARISMA

1 Are leaders born or made? Many leaders throughout history—such as Gandhi, Churchill, Napoleon, and Martin Luther King—seem to have a special quality that made them powerful and persuasive. We can identify that quality as charisma, but can we explain it?

2 Charisma is a complex mixture of social and emotional skills. These skills allow charismatic people to affect and influence others at a deep emotional level, to make strong personal connections, and to communicate effectively with others. Richard Wiseman, a prominent psychologist, points out there are three key attributes of a charismatic person: They feel their own emotions strongly; they inspire strong emotions in other people; and they are unaffected by the influences of other charismatic people.

3 But you shouldn't worry if you don't have these qualities. Charisma used to be thought of as innate, but today there is growing evidence that it can be learned. People with an infectious personality influence others to copy their posture, body language, and facial expressions. Wiseman says that when you come upon someone who has charisma, you mimic his or her posture and facial expressions without realizing it. This is called mirroring, and it works because to some extent, people's behavior influences their emotions. Wiseman adds that you're unaware you're picking up the other person's gestures, but you know it makes you feel good. He cites the example of smiling back at someone who has smiled at you.

4 This type of physical presence can be learned and used to great effect. For example, if you stand up straight and raise your chest, you are more likely to feel confident and inspire others to feel confidence in you. Another expert says that the most charismatic people are good listeners. She cautions that you should ask questions and not try to be the center of attention.

5 Charisma plays a large part in success because it is linked to self-confidence. But it is worth noting that although charisma can be learned, it can't be faked. One successful leadership coach points out that people pick up on that right away. You need to come by your skills and techniques naturally, she warns—if the personality you project is not genuine, you may come across as insincere.

PRACTICE BEING CHARISMATIC

In general: Use an open body posture, keep your hands away from your face when talking, stand up straight, relax, keep your hands apart with palms facing forward or upward

One-on-one: Let people know they matter and you enjoy being with them. Develop a genuine smile, nod when people talk, and maintain eye contact.

In a group: Be comfortable as a leader. Move around to appear enthusiastic, lean slightly forward, and look at everyone in a group.

Your message: Move beyond the ordinary and try to be fresh and make a difference. Be sure your message is easy to understand.

Your speech: Speak clearly, fluently, forcefully, and articulately. Speak in an upbeat manner, but slow down occasionally for emphasis.

Developing critical thinking

Discuss these questions in a group.

1 Think of the charismatic person you considered in the *Before you read* section. Which of the techniques mentioned in the text do they use?

When she speaks, she always ...

2 Do you think charisma can be learned? Why or why not?

Charisma can/can't be learned because ...

READING 2 The healing power of persuasion

Before you read

Discuss these questions with a partner.

1 When was the last time you were sick or injured? What did you do to take care of yourself?

2 Do you use positive thinking to help yourself feel better? Why or why not?

FEELING UNWELL	
go to hospital	stay in bed
see a doctor	take medicine

Global reading

> **BRIDGE SENTENCES**
>
> The first sentence in a paragraph can act as a transition. These are called bridge sentences, and they can be used to introduce another supporting detail, give another example, set up or continue a story, introduce a contrast, or act as a "teaser" to the information that follows. A teaser generates interest for the information that is to come.
>
> Note that bridge sentences are used frequently in less formal text types, but they are less common in academic texts. Learn to recognize them but be cautious about using them in your own academic writing.

1 **Read the opening sentences of each paragraph in *The healing power of persuasion*. Which ones are bridge sentences?**

2 **Find an example of the following in the text:**
   1 a bridge sentence that acts as a "teaser"
   2 a bridge sentence that introduces a contrast
   3 a bridge sentence that sets up a "story"

Close reading

1 **Identify which paragraphs of *The healing power of persuasion* will contain the answers to these questions.**

   1 Can a positive belief about a treatment cause a
      physical response?   Paragraph ___
   2 What is the placebo effect?   Paragraph ___
   3 Does the placebo effect work only for fake medicines?   Paragraph ___
   4 How does trusting their doctor help patients heal?   Paragraph ___
   5 Why is the placebo effect stronger in real situations?   Paragraph ___

2 **Skim *The healing power of persuasion* again and answer the questions in exercise 1.**

3 What are these words referring to? Read *The healing power of persuasion* again and match.

1. it (line 2)
2. that (line 15)
3. did (line 21)
4. subsequent (line 36)
5. the opposite (line 43)
6. its (line 49)
7. ones (line 68)

a. after 1955
b. pulse rates, etc., were lowered
c. the natural cure
d. people's trust in doctors
e. real drugs
f. got better
g. a medical treatment

THE HEALING POWER
OF PERSUASION

1 If you're looking for a natural cure for just about anything, you'll be happy to know there is one. You only need two words to explain how it works: "I believe." The placebo effect—the ability of a fake pill or treatment to make you feel better, just because you are persuaded that it will—is the brain's ability to heal physical symptoms, such as pain, anxiety, and fatigue.

2 Many people go to the doctor's office when they're sick, and often, they leave with a prescription. Most people don't ask questions about what's *in* the medicine the 10 doctor has prescribed. Instead they trust that doctors know what they're doing—they know about the rigorous medical training doctors must complete, and the thorough examination process they have to go through. 15 But how much does that help the healing process? What if, after filling their prescription and taking it as prescribed, patients found out that the medicine the doctor had given them wasn't a real drug? Yet, they did get 20 better. They trusted that they would get well after taking the medicine, so they did.

3 How can a fake medicine help someone to get better? Sensory experience and thoughts can affect the brain, and the brain 25 can affect other systems, including the hormonal and immune systems. Therefore, a person's optimism and hopefulness may be important to his physical recovery from an injury or sickness. Some experts believe that 30 placebos, or fake medicines, simply cause a psychological response. In other words, taking them only enhances your sense of well-being. However, H.K. Beecher found in a revolutionary 1955 study that 32% of 35 patients responded medically to a placebo. Subsequent studies support this finding with specific and measurable results. For example, one study showed that placebos could raise pulse rates, blood 40 pressure, and reaction speed when people were told they had taken a stimulant. When people were told that a medicine would make them drowsy, the opposite occurred.

45 **4** Today, before a drug can be approved, it must be tested and proven more effective than a placebo. Because both a doctor's and a patient's belief in the value of a treatment can affect its outcome, most 50 drug trials are usually double-blind, which means that not only the patients, but also the doctors are unaware of who is receiving a placebo and who is receiving the real drug. Almost all double-blind studies 55 show some benefit to the people taking a placebo, but in actual clinical practice, there is evidence that for some conditions, positive responses to a placebo may be as high as 80 to 90%. The reason is that in a real treatment, 60 the placebo effect is enhanced by the doctor's and the patient's expectations that the treatment will work.

5 But the placebo effect doesn't happen only with fake medicines. Experts say the 65 placebo effect is responsible for about a third of the benefits of *any* treatment—even carefully tested drugs. This means that even effective ones are enhanced by the power of positive thinking. As a result, many people 70 think that doctors should prescribe a placebo when it's appropriate and when the patient's health isn't in danger. According to leading practitioners, the point is to create the right mental state in patients. If up to 30% of 75 patients can get better on cheaper, risk-free placebos, then why not encourage their use?

ACADEMIC KEYWORDS

ability	(n)	/əˈbɪləti/
examination	(n)	/ɪgˌzæmɪˈneɪʃ(ə)n/
subsequent	(adj)	/ˈsʌbsɪkwənt/

Developing critical thinking

1 Discuss these questions in a group.

1. Would prescribing a placebo be a good strategy for these problems? Why or why not?

   a life-threatening injury   a mild headache   an unknown sickness
   early stages of cancer   pain from a back injury   the flu

   It would be a good/bad strategy for … because …

2. Do you think a placebo could ever work for you? Why or why not?

   A placebo might work for me because …

2 **Think about the ideas from *Charisma* and *The healing power of persuasion* and discuss these questions in a group.**

1 If belief in the value of a treatment can affect its outcome, do you think that persuasiveness and charisma are important qualities for medical practitioners? Why or why not? What other professions require charisma?

I think / don't think it's important for doctors to be charismatic because ...

2 If positive thinking promotes good health, do you think charismatic and self-confident people are healthier than people who are less charismatic? Why or why not?

Charismatic people are usually more ... which means ...

Vocabulary skill

FINDING MEANING FROM SYNONYMS OR ANTONYMS

Writers often use several synonyms within a text in order to add variety to the language. When you come across an unfamiliar word, look at the sentences around it. Often, you will find a synonym that will help you guess the meaning of the word you don't know. Sometimes, a contrasting idea or antonym can help you. Look for words like *but*, *however*, and *whereas*.

1 **Find the words below in *Charisma* and *The healing power of persuasion*. Note down the words in the text that can help you guess their meaning.**

1	attributes	*qualities*
2	innate	
3	mimic	
4	insincere	
5	prescription	
6	rigorous	
7	optimism	
8	clinical practice	

2 **Decide if the words you noted down in exercise 1 are synonyms or antonyms, and mark them *S* or *A* accordingly.**

3 **Complete the sentences with the correct form of a word from the left hand column in exercise 1.**

1 Some personality traits of charismatic people can be learned—they're not always _____.

2 If you are fake or _____, people will realize it immediately.

3 One of the most important _____ of charismatic people is that they inspire strong emotions in people.

4 A charismatic person will inspire you to _____ his body language and facial expressions.

5 When a doctor gives you a _____, do you care if the drug is real or not?

6 The high degree of effectiveness of placebos in _____ practice proves that _____ can help you heal.

7 A doctor with _____ medical training should know when it's not a good strategy to prescribe a placebo.

WRITING Writing a persuasive essay

You are going to learn about presenting a claim and using indirect quotation.
You are then going to use these to write a paragraph presenting a claim with
your own ideas and the ideas of your classmates.

Writing skill

▪ PRESENTING A CLAIM ▪

A claim is a statement that can be argued. A persuasive text begins with a claim about a topic that people could have differing opinions about. In order for your text to be effective, your claim must be specific. A topic that is too broad leaves open too many questions for the writer to address in one text.

An effective claim must be backed up by supporting examples and details. In order to persuade readers, you should vary the types of supporting details. Try to use at least one example, logical explanation, expert opinion, and statistic. You don't need to use each type in every text, but varying the types of support makes your work more interesting to read.

1 Read the main ideas with a partner. Which ones would be most suitable for a five-paragraph text? Cross-out the ideas that are too broad.

- Advertisements for medicines that appear on TV, in magazines, and on the radio can't be trusted.
- Celebrities who appear in ads for medicines can't be trusted because they are paid.
- Doctors shouldn't prescribe placebos in life-threatening situations.
- Doctors should never prescribe placebos.
- Patients should never trust the medicines their doctors prescribe.
- Patients should always get a second medical opinion before taking a medication.

2 Choose one main idea in exercise 1. With a partner, come up with a supporting sentence for each type of support.

1 example
2 logical explanation
3 expert opinion (can be made up)
4 statistic (can be made up)

Grammar

INDIRECT QUOTATION

Indirect quotation is used to talk about what another person says, thinks, or believes, without quoting that person directly. We do not use their exact words. In academic texts and articles that give general information and facts, the present tense is usually used.

Some common reporting verbs are: *say, ask, add, point out, think, believe, warn, explain.*

Quoted speech	Indirect quotation
"People usually mimic the posture, body language, and facial expressions of someone with charisma."	A prominent psychologist **says that** people mimic the posture and facial expressions of a charismatic person.
"You aren't aware you're mimicking, but you know it makes you feel a certain way—happy."	The doctor **added that** you're unaware you're mimicking the person, but you know it makes you feel good.
"Although you can learn to be charismatic, you can't fake it."	Although charisma can be learned, one leadership coach **pointed out**, it can't be faked.

1 **Change the direct quotes to indirect quotation, using the reporting verb in parentheses. Do not use the exact words in the quote.**

1 Dr. Smith said, "Charismatic people usually lean forward and make eye contact with everyone in the group." (point out)

2 "People like taking a placebo because it works," a leading doctor said, "and they tend to get better, too." (explain)

3 "In drug trials, researchers have to be sure that a drug works better than a placebo," one scientist said. "Otherwise, the drug doesn't get approved." (add)

4 "Placebos and fake medicines simply cause a psychological response, they do not actually have any direct effect on the body," claimed Barnett. (believe)

5 Johnson said, "People tend to copy the behavior of charismatic people subconsciously in a number of ways, including mimicking body language." (think)

6 One leading researcher stated, "You can learn charisma, but you cannot fake it." (warn)

2 **Work with a partner. Take turns making statements about information in the texts and writing them down as indirect quotation.**

Placebos are cheaper and don't involve any risks.

My partner pointed out that placebos cost less and are risk-free.

WRITING TASK

Write a persuasive essay about public speaking.

BRAINSTORM

1 Read the excerpt from a persuasive essay, highlight the topic sentence, underline the supporting detail, and circle any reporting verb.

Homeopathic or "natural" medicines are a very profitable business, but they are actually no more effective than placebos. Millions of dollars are spent every year on these treatments, and millions of people swear that they work. However, many prominent scientists believe that the main reason they work is the placebo effect—patients get better because they believe they will. A study by Dr. P. MacDonald showed that in a trial, 53% of people using a homeopathic treatment got better within a week, but 52% of people using a placebo showed the same improvements. On the other hand, 73% of people using a non-homeopathic drug were cured. This provides very strong evidence that homeopathic medicines are no more effective than a placebo, Dr. MacDonald claims.

2 You are going to write a 2–3-paragraph essay about whether or not you can learn to be a good public speaker. Think about the types of support you will need to back up your claim.

GATHER INFORMATION

Poll several classmates. Ask them to share their personal opinions and experiences about the topic. Write down what they say.

PLAN

Plan your essay. Look back at your brainstorm and write a topic sentence. Decide how you want to organize each paragraph. Can you use statistics from your poll as supporting details? (For example, 20% of people interviewed felt …)

WRITE

Write a paragraph introducing your claim and the main argument(s) supporting it. Then write the next two paragraphs, paying attention to your paragraph structure, especially the supporting details. Try to provide examples using reported speech. Your essay should be 200–250 words long.

SHARE

Exchange essays with a partner. Look at the checklist on page 109 and provide feedback to your partner.

REWRITE AND EDIT

Consider your partner's comments and rewrite your essay.

Critical thinking when writing

by Stella Cottrell

Critical thinking when *writing* includes most of the elements of critical thinking when *reading*. It can be more difficult to analyze your own work critically, however, and to recognize and admit to your own opinions and bias.

Students' writing is often weakened because their thinking is not clear before they start to write their final draft. This is partly a question of planning, and partly a question of spending enough time on critical analysis. It is important to spend time evaluating both what you have read, and your own ideas and writing.

Be clear about your conclusions

It is surprising how often students hand in work which shows that although they have done the necessary reading and even given their work considerable thought, they are not sure of their conclusions. The whole of the piece of writing should lead to its conclusion: if the conclusions are vague or understated, all of the writing loses its force.

As soon as you are given a piece of work to do, write down what you think your conclusion will be. Put this where you can see it. Whenever you find out something that requires you to revise or adjust your conclusion, write out a new one. This may seem like doing things the wrong way around, but your writing will be clearer if you write your conclusions first.

Have a clear line of reasoning

If your conclusions are clear, your argument or line of reasoning is likely to be clear also. If you are playing soccer, you need to know where the goal is so you can aim the ball. Your conclusion is like the goal—it shows you where you need to direct your line of reasoning.

Keep your writing focused.

Bear in mind four guidelines:

1 Early drafts may be helpful in elaborating and refining your thinking. However, be sure that your final version says what you really think.

2 Work to a writing plan which sets out the reasons, examples, and evidence in the most logical order.

3 Consider how best to link ideas and pieces of information, so that your writing is not just a list of facts but a line of reasoning.

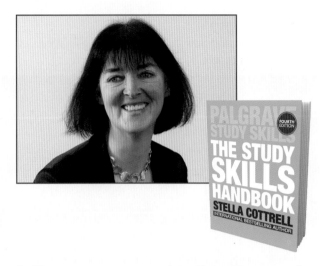

4 Keep your argument clear. From the mass of information gathered at the research stage, select the points that best support your argument and indicate them clearly.

Use evidence to support your reasoning

Use evidence selectively: too many examples may make it difficult to see your line of reasoning. Choose a few items that clearly support your case.

Evaluate your own writing through critical reading

As a student, you also have "readers." Your tutors or examiners will take a critical reading approach when marking your work. Examine your own writing in the same way you would examine someone else's, as outlined above.

Look at things from different points of view

Whether you are reading, listening, observing, or writing, you will be expected to be able to analyze your own and others' arguments—and indeed work, designs, or proposals—from more than one perspective. This will mean considering *both* their good *and* their bad points, *both* their strengths *and* their weaknesses.

When you think critically and analyze things from several perspectives, the answer is rarely a straightforward one of right or wrong. Usually there are many contradictory pieces of evidence to weigh up and evaluate against each other.

PALGRAVE
STUDY SKILLS

———— FROM BESTSELLING AUTHOR STELLA COTTRELL ————

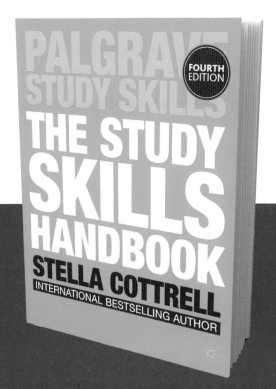

"... it was really difficult reading and taking notes at the beginning of the first term. After having read this book, I found [out] how to improve my reading speed and to make good notes. Therefore, I strongly recommend this book"
- International student studying in the U.K.

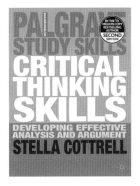
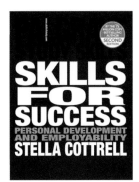

——— www.palgravestudyskills.com ———

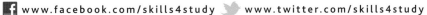 www.facebook.com/skills4study www.twitter.com/skills4study

The phrases below give common ways of expressing useful functions. Use them to help you as you're completing the *Discussion points* and *Developing critical thinking* activities.

Asking for clarification

Sorry, can you explain that some more?
Could you say that another way?
When you say … do you mean …?
Sorry, I don't follow that.
What do you mean?

Asking for repetition

Could you repeat that, please?
I'm sorry, I didn't catch that.
Could you say that again?

When you don't know the word for something

What does … mean?
Sorry, I'm not sure what … means.

Working with a partner

Would you like to start?
Shall I go first?
Shall we do this one first?
Where do you want to begin?

Giving opinions

I think that …
It seems to me that …
In my opinion …
As I see it …

Agreeing and disagreeing

I know what you mean.
That's true.
You have a point there.
Yes. I see what you're saying, but …
I understand your point, but …
I don't think that's true.

Asking for opinions

Do you think …?
Do you feel …?
What do you think about …?
How about you, Jennifer? What do you think?
What about you?
Does anyone have any other ideas?
Do you have any thoughts on this?

Asking for more information

In what way?
Why do you think that?
Can you give an example?

Not giving a strong preference

It doesn't matter to me.
I don't really have a strong preference.
I've never really thought about that.
Either is fine.

Expressing interest

I'd like to hear more about that.
That sounds interesting.
How interesting!
Tell me more about that.

Giving reasons

This is … because …
This has to be … because …
I think … because …

Checking understanding

Do you know what I mean?
Do you see what I'm saying?
Are you following me?

Putting things in order

This needs to come first because …
I think this is the most/least important because …
For me, this is the most/least relevant because …

Preventing interruptions

Excuse me, I wasn't finished.
If I could just finish what I was saying …
Let me just finish this, please.
I haven't finished my thought/sentence.

Buying time

Let me think about that for a moment.
Let me gather my thoughts.
Just a minute. I need to think about that.

Clarifying

That's not exactly what I meant.
Sorry, I wasn't clear. Let me put it another way.
That isn't what I was trying to say.

Writing task peer review checklist

Use the checklist below as you read over your partner's work.

PROCESS WRITING CHECKLIST

1 Does the paragraph have these things:

name ☐
class ☐
the date ☐
a title ☐

2 Could you follow the main idea of the paragraph? Is it a good response to the writing assignment?

3 Does every sentence begin and end with correct punctuation? Is every paragraph indented?

4 What is your favorite sentence or point from the paragraph?

5 Did you notice any target vocabulary from the unit? Write it here:

_____

6 Highlight any target grammar from the unit.

7 <u>Underline</u> the topic sentence or sentences.

8 Write one question about the paragraph for the writer.

The publishers would like to thank the following for their thoughtful insights and perceptive comments during the development of the material:

Belgium

Sylviane Granger, at CECL, University of Louvain
Magali Paquot

Egypt

Dr. Gaber Khalil, AUC, Cairo
Heidi Omara

Germany

John Nixon at Universität Stuttgart

Ireland

Fiodhna Gardiner-Hyland at University of Limerick

Japan

Robert Morton at Chuo University
Lesley Burda Ito

Oman

Mutaz Abumuaath at Nizwa College of Technology, Nizwa

Qatar

Jane Hoelker at Qatar University, Foundation English

Saudi Arabia

Dr. Mohammed Hamdan, Imam Muhammad Ibn Saud University
Mohammed AL-Ahaydib, Imam University
William Frawley, Education Experts

South Korea

Yoonji Kim, and Da young Song at the Konkuk University Language Institute
Jina Kwon at Seoul National University

Taiwan

Laura Wang at Chung Yuan Christian University
Regina Jan at Lunghwa University of Science and Technology
Kitty Chu, Jessie Huang, Jenny Jen, and Wenyau Keng at the National Central University, Language Center
Sandrine Ting at the Department of Applied Foreign Language, St. John's University

Thailand

Sureepan Thepud, Nattinee Khueansri, Nongluck Srivichai, and Penporn Jatuworapruk at Payap University
Wanpen Chaikitmongkol, Jindarat De Vleeschauwer, and Sonhsi Wichaidit at the English Division, Department of Western Languages and Humanities, Chiang Mai University

Turkey

Merve Oflaz at Bahcesehir University
Şahika Özkan-Tuğba Kın-Yadigar Aslan, Didem Gümüşlüoğlu, Meltem Sarandal, and Sibel Weeks at Doğuş University, İstanbul
Sevil Altıkulaçoğlu, Sühendan Semine Er, Şerife Ersöz, Fatma Ünveren Gürocak at Gazi University
Deniz Ateşok at Istanbul Bilgi University
Ebru Yamaç at Maltepe University,
Aybike Oğuz at Özyeğin University

United Arab Emirates

Paul Barney, Doug Henderson, and Danielle Norris at Higher Colleges of Technology, Al Ain

United Kingdom

Nick Hillman at Anglia Ruskin University
Heather Abel and Richard Hillman at Bell London
Edward Bressan, Sara Hannam, and Stacey Hughes at Oxford Brookes University
Sally Morris, Ian Pople, and Simon Raw at University of Manchester
Averil Bolster and Peter Levrai at University of Nottingham, Ningbo
Jonathan Hadley
Jane Neill at University of Gloucestershire

United States

Gail Schafers at Fontbonne Univeristy
Carole Mawson at Stanford University
Denise Mussman at University of Missouri
Abby Brown

Macmillan Education
4 Crinan Street
London N1 9XW
A division of Macmillan Publishers Limited
Companies and representatives throughout the world

ISBN 978-0-230-42986-4

Text, design and illustration © Macmillan Publishers Limited 2013
Written by Louis Rogers and Jennifer Wilkin
Series Consultant Dorothy E. Zemach

The authors have asserted their rights to be identified as the author/s
of this work in accordance with the Copyright, Design and Patents Act
1988.

First published 2013

Designed by emc design ltd
Illustrated by emc design ltd
Cover design by emc design ltd
Cover illustration/photograph by Getty/Thinkstock
Picture research by Emily Taylor

The Academic Keyword List (AKL) was designed by Magali Paquot at
the Centre for English Corpus Linguistics, Université catholique de
Louvain (Belgium) within the framework of a research project led by
Professor Sylviane Granger.

http://www.uclouvain.be/en-372126.html

Authors' acknowledgements

Louis Rogers
I'd like to thank Jennifer Wilkin and everyone at Macmillan for their
help and support in developing this course. I also thank my family for
their support throughout my career.

Jennifer Wilkin
I acknowledge and thank Louis John Rogers and the team at
Macmillan for their generous support during the writing process. I
also thank my parents, who instilled a love of language via nature and
nurture, and my daughter Lily, who keeps clear my perspective.

The authors and publishers would like to thank the following for
permission to reproduce their photographs:

Alamy/Art of Food p15(tr), Alamy/Vicki Beaver p68(tr), Alamy/
Classic Image p79(cr), Alamy/David Cook p102, Alamy/GL Archive
p79(tr), Alamy/Ivy Close Images p85, Alamy/Mary Evans Picture
Library p53(cr), Alamy/David Pearson p75, Alamy/Pictorial Press Ltd
p98(bcr), Alamy/Radius Images p79(background), Alamy/Tetra Images
p52, Alamy/A.T. Willett p54(bcr);

Axiom Photographic/Robert Caputo p77, Axiom Photographic/Beth
Wald p9;

BrandX p44;

Comstock Images p54(tr);

Corbis p88, Corbis/Atlantide Phototravel pp37, 80(br), Corbis/Gary
Bell p91, Corbis/Bettmann p51, Corbis/Blue Images p96, Corbis/
Fabio Cardoso p23, Corbis/Miloslav Druckmuller/Science Faction
p29, Corbis/Fosten p60, Corbis/Kennet Havgaard p19, Corbis/
Hannes Hepp p70, Corbis/Aaron Horowitz p31, Corbis/James Leynse
p48(4), Corbis/Louis Moses, Corbis/Laurence Mouton p105, Corbis/
NASA p27, Corbis/Ocean pp13, 62, 74(bm), 100, Corbis/Micha
Pawlitzki p84, Corbis/Monty Rakusen p59, Corbis/Roger Ressmeyer
p30, Corbis/Christian Richters p74(cr), Corbis/Boris Roessler/dpa
p57, Corbis/Hugh Sitton p15(cm), Corbis/Visuals Unlimited p53(bm);
FotoLibra/Sherri Carnson p78, FotoLibra/Philip Carr p98(br),
FotoLibra/John Cleare p42, FotoLibra/James Fowler p54(tcr),
FotoLibra/Stanley Partlett p10, FotoLibra/Walter Rawlings pp40,
45(tr), FotoLibra/Ana Sundman p45(tl), FotoLibra/Paul Taylor p25;
Getty Images pp32, 48(3), 48(1), 54(br), 56, 64(tr), 92, Getty Images/
AFP pp48(5), 95, Getty Images/Barry Austin Photography p55, Getty
Images/Merce Bellera p66, Getty Images/Bloomberg p48(6), Getty
Images/Gary Benson p22, Getty Images/Blend Images p26, Getty
Images/Compassionate Eye Foundation/Steven Errico p12(tr), Getty
Images/Cultura pp12(br), 98(tr), Getty Images/Erik Dreyer p93, Getty
Images/EschCollection p38, Getty Images/Flickr RF pp21, 83, Getty
Images/Flickr RM p24, Getty Images/Edward Freeman p72, Getty
Images/Steve Granitz p48(7), Getty Images/Hindustan Times p48(8),
Getty Images/Hulton Archive p98(cr), Getty Images/The Image
Bank p68(br), Getty Images/Abid Katib p47, Getty Images/Jonathan
Kitchen p58, Getty Images/Catherine Ledner p80(tr), Getty Images/
David Madison p49, Getty Images/David Malan p87, Getty Images/
Win McNamee p48(2), Getty Images/Ryan Mcvay p69, Getty Images/
Jim Naughten p64(br), Getty Images/OJO Images pp18, 86, Getty
Images/Popperfoto p97, Getty Images/David Robbins p65, Getty
Images/Jeff Rotman p67, Getty Images/Stone+ p17, Getty Images/
Babek Tafreshi p35, Getty Images/Bob Thomas p104, Getty Images/
Time & Life Pictures p99, Getty Images/Zomi p11;

John Foxx Images p94;

Photodisc p33;

Plain Picture/Cultura p90, Plain Picture/Neuebildanstalt p7, Plain
Picture/OJO p43;

Press Association Images/The Canadian Press pp28(tr), (cr).

The author(s) and publishers are grateful for permission to reprint the
following copyright material

Material from 'The Study Skills Handbook' by author Stella Cottrell,
copyright © Stella Cottrell 1999, 2003 & 2008, first published by
Palgrave Macmillan, reproduced with permission of the publisher.

These materials may contain links for third party websites. We have
no control over, and are not responsible for, the contents of such third
party websites. Please use care when accessing them.

Although we have tried to trace and contact copyright holders before
publication, in some cases this has not been possible. If contacted
we will be pleased to rectify any errors or omissions at the earliest
opportunity.

Printed and bound in Thailand

2018 2017 2016 2015 2014
10 9 8 7 6 5 4 3

Skillful **Digibook**

For recommended system requirements, visit **Help** at www.skillfuldigibooks.com